THE JOY THIEF

THE JOY THIEF

How OCD steals your happiness—
and how to get it back

PENNY MOODIE

ALLEN&UNWIN
SYDNEY·MELBOURNE·AUCKLAND·LONDON

First published in 2023

Allen & Unwin
Cammeraygal Country
83 Alexander Street
Crows Nest NSW 2065
Australia
Phone: (61 2) 8425 0100
Email: info@allenandunwin.com
Web: www.allenandunwin.com

Allen & Unwin acknowledges the Traditional Owners of the Country on which we live and work. We pay our respects to all Aboriginal and Torres Strait Islander Elders, past and present.

A catalogue record for this book is available from the National Library of Australia

ISBN 978 1 76106 866 9

Author photo by Sally Goodall
Set in 11.6/18.8 pt Sabon LT Pro by Bookhouse, Sydney
Printed and bound in Australia by the Opus Group

10 9 8 7 6 5 4

For my mum, Anne,
who never stopped trying to understand

CONTENTS

PREFACE

'You understand the pain and frustration of being locked in
a strange world in which you know that your thoughts and
behaviors make no sense. It is as if you have simultaneously
lost your mind and, at the same time, are so sane that you
are a witness to the loss.'

Dr Jonathan Grayson, *Freedom from Obsessive-Compulsive Disorder*[1]

The only thing worse than suffering a mental illness is suffering
a mental illness without knowing what it is. I wasn't officially
diagnosed with obsessive-compulsive disorder (OCD) until four
years ago, when I was 31. For so many years I thought I was
overly anxious at best, and completely insane at worst. I didn't
recognise the obsessive and compulsive patterns my mind was
following, because all I understood about OCD was that it

was an illness that drove people to wash their hands until they bled. That's how I'd seen it depicted in movies, books and TV shows. But that's not how my OCD played out, so it didn't occur to me that I was suffering from a serious mental illness that needed treatment. This resulted in years of distress and anguish, and a huge amount of pressure being placed on me (trying to get better on my own) and on my family (as I turned to them for reassurance).

One of the reasons I wanted to write this book was to help people make sense of their experiences, because there's still so much confusion surrounding OCD. Until there's widespread and comprehensive understanding of OCD among the public and, importantly, health professionals, people will continue to suffer for far longer than they should. Currently, the average time between the onset of symptoms and a diagnosis of OCD is nine years,[2] although some studies have shown it to be up to seventeen years.[3] That lengthy period stuck in the OCD cycle feels like a lifetime, and the longer it takes to find help, the more ingrained the obsessive patterns become in your mind.

You can't be expected to fight effectively if you don't know anything about your opponent. You're essentially fighting blind, swinging your arms wildly, hoping you'll land a punch, but getting knocked down on most occasions and completely knocked out on others. I've largely been in the ring by myself, fighting this unknown adversary, but I'm lucky that I've had a supportive family cheering me on and helping me to get up each time I've hit the canvas. I worry for those who are in the arena alone, without anyone in their corner who can pick them up. I hope that by openly sharing my knowledge and delving into all facets of this illness with experts and those with lived experience, it will help people with OCD find the answers they so desperately need.

NOTE TO THOSE WITH OCD

None of this is your fault. With OCD, it's like you're dealing with dysfunctional machinery. But you as a person are anything BUT dysfunctional. You're working overtime to keep your head above water. You try to stay afloat when the intrusive thoughts and compulsions are trying to pull you into the throes of insanity. In a sense, you're living a double life: one inside your head, and the other trying to appear functional to the outside world. This is exhausting. Bone-achingly exhausting.

Believe it or not, your thoughts aren't the problem. Everyone, everywhere, has weird, disturbing, dark, unsettling thoughts. *Everyone.* The thing that's causing you so much distress is the behaviours that are being used to regulate the emotions that the thoughts have stirred up. Once you learn how to change your behaviours, the distress will diminish. The thoughts won't go away, because we can never control our thoughts. But you'll learn how to live with all kinds of thoughts (any kinds of thoughts!) without engaging in compulsive behaviours. You'll finally be able to give yourself permission to step out of the OCD hell you've been living in and fully immerse yourself in the real world, where uncertainty is always present—AND that's okay.

This probably sounds so ridiculously far-fetched that you might be questioning *my* sanity. I get it. But I want to assure you that I've been where you are. I may not have been reacting to the same thoughts or engaging in the same behaviours, but I've sat in the depths of despair, driven to insanity, wondering if I'd be stuck in this diabolical labyrinth of mental illness forever. And once I was finally diagnosed with OCD, it felt like I'd been given a map that showed me how to escape the maze.

The good news is that the main treatment for OCD— exposure and response prevention (ERP)—is extremely effective, and more and more therapists around the world are becoming better equipped to provide ERP to their clients. This isn't to say that ERP is the only tool that should be used in treatment; however, there's overwhelming evidence that suggests it's the most powerful.

I hope, more than anything, that this book provides you with some relief. You're not bad. You're not dangerous. You're not crazy. And you're certainly not alone. You're incredible.

And you deserve a break.

Chapter 1

THE ONSET

I've spent a lot of my life sitting on toilet seats. My earliest memory of spending an awkward amount of time shut in a cubicle was when I was six years old. My older brother, Nick, was knocking impatiently on the door, because he was busting for a wee. Sick of waiting for a response, he barged in.

'What are you doing? You're not even going to the toilet!' he exclaimed. I was sitting on the toilet lid with my eyes tightly shut.

'Sorry excuse me, sorry excuse me,' I whispered in a barely audible voice.

'What? . . . No, it's okay. I'm just busting, so can you get out?'

'Sorry excuse me, sorry excuse me,' I continued chanting.

'Pen, what are you doing? Snap out of it!'

Barely hearing him, I finally opened my eyes—satisfied that I was done and could now move on with the rest of my day. 'I did a burp, and I needed to say sorry,' I said in a matter-of-fact tone to try to hide my embarrassment.

'Say sorry to who?' Nick asked.

'Just say sorry . . . you know . . . so the police won't come.'

'Wait . . . what?' My much more mature and logical eight-year-old brother didn't even know where to begin with my outlandish declaration that I'd be arrested for burping, so he just shook his head and gently nudged me towards the door.

It wasn't only the fear of being arrested that had begun to plague me. At the age of six or seven, I started to worry that if my parents went out for dinner, they wouldn't come back. They might be in a horrific car accident, and the babysitter would have to wake me and my brother in the middle of the night to break the news to us. This is a very normal fear for a young kid to have. We rely so much on our parents that the thought of them suddenly not being there is overwhelming. But instead of worrying about it for a bit, and then being distracted by a fart joke or watching a cartoon on TV, I started to develop compulsions such as tapping on wood a certain number of times and repeating specific phrases in a precise order in my head before I went to sleep. In my mind, if I didn't carry out these compulsions, my parents would not come home. I don't really understand why these specific compulsions developed. I'd seen people knock on wood after saying something that scared them, and, in my mind, repeating phrases in my head somehow signalled a message to the universe: *make these people safe.* Their safety suddenly became my responsibility.

That's a large burden to shoulder for someone who couldn't yet tie her own shoelaces.

Little did I know that over the next 25 years I'd spend a lot more time sitting on toilet seats, eyes closed, head in hands, trying to 'work things out' or 'make things right' (I quickly learned to lock bathroom doors). I became that annoying girl who'd take a stupid amount of time to go to the toilet at nightclubs and music festivals. But the people on the other side of the toilet door weren't quite as patient as my brother was. I heard some variation of the phrase 'GET OUT ALREADY, YOU STUPID MOLE' more times than I'd liked. But obsessive-compulsive disorder (OCD) will do that. It will humiliate you and put you in hideously cringeworthy situations. And you'll endure it, because the fear of your thoughts and the dread of uncertainty will always override your embarrassment or pride.

SQUASHED BANANAS

It was 1994, and we were sitting in our favourite Italian family restaurant, which was famous for its speedy service and outrageously generous ice-cream servings. (It would later be known for being slapped with a $3000 fine for having a cockroach-infested kitchen.) While we were waiting for our enormous pizzas to come out, my parents asked my brother and me, in a very casual tone, how we would feel about leaving Melbourne to live in Geneva, Switzerland, for three years. My dad had

What is OCD?

OCD is characterised by the presence of obsessions and/or compulsions. Obsessions are recurrent, persistent and intrusive thoughts, images or urges, which cause the person experiencing them significant distress.[1] Compulsions are repetitive behaviours, which can be either physical (e.g. checking, washing or touching routines) or mental (e.g. counting, ruminating or replaying past actions). Compulsions are performed in response to obsessions, to neutralise the anxiety that obsessions provoke or to prevent a feared outcome from occurring. It's important to point out that while compulsions tend to offer temporary relief, these actions aren't done for pleasure,[2] and they can be extremely tiring and inconvenient.

One of the criteria used to help distinguish OCD from occasional intrusive thoughts or repetitive behaviours is that the obsessions and compulsions must be time-consuming, or cause significant distress or impairment.[3] Across the world, current estimates suggest that OCD affects 1.1–1.8 per cent of the population.[4] To put that into perspective, it means around 470,000 Australians experience OCD. More men are affected by childhood OCD, while a slightly higher number of women experience OCD in adulthood.[5]

OCD had long been included in the Anxiety Disorder section of the *Diagnostic and Statistical Manual of Mental Disorders* (DSM), but in the Fifth Edition it appears in a different category: Obsessive Compulsive and Related Disorders.[6] OCD-related disorders include hoarding disorder, trichotillomania (hair-pulling disorder), body dysmorphic disorder and dermatillomania (skin-picking disorder), among others.[7] In this book, I'm not going to discuss any of these related disorders—I will be talking solely about OCD.

OCD can present in a variety of ways, known as subtypes or common themes. Don't fret if your subtype isn't listed in the table below. With OCD, it's not so much about the content of your obsessions, but how you respond to them. Some people will suffer from different themes at once, and it's common for them to change over time.

Common OCD themes	Examples
Contamination	Fears of viruses, germs, dirt, bodily fluids, asbestos, chemicals etc. Emotional contamination also occurs when people fear that thinking or talking about a disease can contaminate someone.
Existential	Constantly questioning the meaning or reality of life or one's own existence.
Danger	Fearing that something bad will happen to you or those around you. These obsessions are often teamed with checking rituals; for example, checking the oven is turned off or the door is locked.
Relationship	Frequently questioning the 'rightness' of a relationship.
Sexual Orientation	Fearing that you don't know for sure what your sexual orientation is.

Common OCD themes	Examples
Magical Thinking	Fearing that you will be responsible for something bad happening if you don't perform certain actions or rituals. There is often no logical connection between the fear and the action or ritual.
Harm	Obsessing that you've harmed someone or that you want to harm yourself or someone else.
Paedophilia	Fearing that you might be a paedophile.
Moral Scrupulosity	Fearing that you aren't living in line with your personal beliefs.
Perinatal	Obsessions that centre around a newborn (or yet to be born) baby. The fears could be around harming the baby, losing the baby or the baby becoming unwell.

been offered a job at the World Health Organization and, even though the decision had clearly been made, they were the kind of parents who made us feel like we had a say.

My dad worked in international health, and we had already moved around a lot by that stage, so the news didn't come as a big shock. My brother and I already knew the drill—new home, new school and new language. I'm not sure about my brother, but I was excited about a new adventure. Also, I had a bowl of gelati the size of my head to look forward to, so I was pretty keen to wrap up the conversation.

Within months, we were unpacking our things in a light-filled fifth-floor apartment in the worldwide centre of diplomacy, Geneva.

Many of my childhood memories are set against a backdrop of being in transit: updating passport photos, packing and unpacking boxes, sitting in airports, fighting over window seats, and watching the lights of new cities morph into view through the clouds. While I relished being in this kind of perpetual motion as a child, it always brought with it unsettling worries that would bubble up and overshadow my excitement. I remember watching a movie called *Nell* on the plane on the way to Geneva. It included some bizarre and unnerving scenes that were probably far too mature for a seven-year-old, and I could barely sleep for the next month.

Each night after arriving in Geneva, I'd discuss the scenes with my mum to try to erase them from my mind. It probably seemed like a little person expressing normal fears, but in retrospect I believe that it was an early example of my mind attaching too much importance to a thought or image. Any time I had a thought that was unusual or unpleasant, I started to worry that I was stuck with it forever.

Eventually, the disconcerting scenes started to blur as I was distracted by the novelty of wearing ski suits to school when the weather dropped below 0 degrees Celsius, and the fact that we had a video shop on the ground floor of our apartment building (most of the videos were in French, but that didn't stop me from watching a dubbed version of Robin Williams' masterpiece *Flubber* ten times).

What is OCPD?

You may not have heard of obsessive-compulsive personality disorder (OCPD), but it's worth understanding the differences between OCPD and OCD. OCPD is a personality disorder that is underpinned by perfectionism and a rigidity in relation to rules and regulations. Around 2–8 per cent of the population are thought to have OCPD, making it one of the most prevalent personality disorders.[8] Twice as many men as women are diagnosed with OCPD. Those with anxiety disorders and OCD are at an increased risk of developing OCPD.

Symptoms of OCPD include:[9]

- excessive fixation with orderliness, rules, details and schedules
- perfectionism that affects the completion of tasks
- preoccupation with work to the extent that it interferes with social/family life
- rigid moral and ethical codes
- hoarding behaviours
- inability to assign tasks to others unless they do things with the same level of detail
- extreme frugality.

Differences between OCD and OCPD[10]

- While those with OCD generally understand that their thoughts and compulsions are illogical or unreasonable, those with OCPD believe that their behaviour is warranted and the 'right' way to do things.

- The obsessions and compulsions that those with OCD experience are usually removed from everyday life, while people with OCPD are fixated on managing everyday activities.
- Those with OCPD generally don't feel as though they require treatment.

Treatment[11]

- cognitive behavioural therapy (CBT), which can increase the level of insight a person has into their rigid behaviours
- medication
- relaxation techniques.

Later, while I was helping Mum look for a more spacious apartment, we came across one that was perfect—close to the international school that my brother and I attended, and within walking distance of Parc Bertrand, a leafy park where surly Swiss dames would take their bewildered-looking chihuahuas out for a trot. I was ecstatic about the prospect of living there, until I had an unusual thought about the blinds: *They look like the colour of squished bananas. From now on, whenever you think of this apartment, all you'll see is mouldy, squashed-up bananas.*

I'm not sure why this thought caused me so much distress, but my mind continued to taunt me. I tried to convince my mum that we needed to find another apartment. 'This one just has a weird . . . feeling? The bathroom's too small! THIS

APARTMENT DOESN'T HAVE A VIDEO SHOP BELOW IT!' Despite my objections, we did indeed rent that apartment. Once I'd confessed to Mum my weird dislike of the blinds, she tried to assure me that the thought would eventually disappear, and to redirect my mind to something more palatable to associate with the colour: sunshine . . . sunflowers . . . Greg, the yellow Wiggle.

None of it seemed to help, and I was sure that any time I was in the apartment my mind would be stuck thinking about mouldy, rotting bananas.

STUCK THOUGHTS

Clinical psychologist Cassie Lavell, co-director at the Centre for Anxiety & OCD (CAO) on the Gold Coast, works primarily with children and adolescents. She uses the term 'stuck thoughts' when she talks to clients about persistent thoughts.

'As adults we might call it intrusive thoughts or repetitive thoughts, but for kids, we call it stuck thoughts—thoughts that just come, and then they hang around and they won't go away,' says Lavell. 'Kids might experience stuck thoughts about germs, sexual obsessions or worries about harm.'

She reiterates that there's nothing abnormal about any of these thoughts. Both kids and adults experience weird and distressing thoughts, but the difference with someone who has OCD is that they find it very hard to move on from these thoughts when they arise.

'Other people might just have that intrusive thought as a kid and go, "Oh, that's a bit weird." Then they just move on and ignore it. But because of the neurobiological factors facing people with OCD, we think those thoughts are more likely to linger and get stuck. And then that's when you attach the meaning, the overvaluation, and you go, "Why am I having this thought? What does that mean?"

'And then the anxiety that comes from that drives the compulsions,' continues Lavell. 'For kids, this could be reassurance-seeking. It could be saying to their mum, "I have this thought—does that mean I'm going to do this awful thing? Does it mean I want that?" They're trying to make meaning of that stuck thought, because it's very confusing to them.'

A NEW PHASE

During the first year of living in the apartment in Geneva, the nature of my fears began to transform. My standard fears of doing the wrong thing, losing my parents or being stuck with a horrible image morphed into a fear of contracting the deadly AIDS virus. Just a subtle change of pace from squashed bananas to AIDS.

Looking back, it's not surprising that this fear sprang up. My dad was working for UNAIDS as the inaugural Director of Country Support. To my eternal embarrassment, his work tie of choice had cartoon-style condoms with faces on it, and he would often talk openly about the importance of safe sex and the devastating consequences of AIDS in developing countries, particularly for women and children.

One chilly December evening, while I was struggling through my French homework on the dining-room table, I started to pay close attention to the story mum was watching on the CNN evening news. It was about a patient who was near the end of their AIDS battle, and they showed him, emaciated and gasping for air, in a hospital bed. I was only eight, and the image was particularly confronting. I'd heard a lot about AIDS, but I had never seen a face associated with the disease. The news segment was over, and the anchor had moved on to informing us about Michael Jackson's collapse on stage in New York. But my mind wasn't moving on. It was suddenly very stuck.

What if I have AIDS? I asked myself. A pang of fear ran through my body. I lost any appetite I previously had for dinner and went to bed that night unable to get the image of the dying man out of my mind. After a few days the fear settled, but it returned a couple of weeks later.

I was on school camp, somewhere in the French country-side, and I was crippled with homesickness. Any time I felt overwhelmed, I would take myself off to the bathroom. On the second night, between the communal dinner and the evening activities, I wandered to the bathroom to wallow in feelings of unease and a deep longing for home. After getting up from the toilet seat, knowing I needed to get back to the dinner hall before anyone noticed I was taking too long, I looked down and saw what appeared to be a small drop of blood on the seat. I knew it wasn't my blood. The AIDS thought immediately resurfaced, but this time it was more of a statement than a question. *The blood is infected with HIV, and it has entered my bloodstream through a tiny cut on my leg or my bottom.*

I felt panicked, and to make things worse, this idea mingled insidiously with another guilty thought I'd been having. When I was a few years younger I'd sometimes played a 'mums and dads' game with my friends, and we would pretend to be in love and sometimes simulate kissing or lie in bed together. I'd forgotten this innocent foray into the mysterious adult world, but when the memories resurfaced, I felt a burning shame. Because of my new fears around contracting AIDS, I started to worry that these experimentations had caused me to contract the deadly disease. Looking back, it's completely illogical, but at the time, the combination of fear, shame and uncertainty was potent. It was as if my brain was crammed with TNT, and someone had taken a match to it. For the rest of the camp, an explosion of what-ifs went off. Little did I know that explosions would continue to fire off for the next 25 years.

The thought of contracting a deadly disease, particularly when one of your parents is deeply immersed in the topic, isn't unusual for a child or an adult. What became unusual was how I dealt with the fearful thoughts: I began to incessantly seek reassurance. I started to talk to my mum about all the ways I could have contracted the disease, and at first her assurances were like a soothing balm on cracked, sore skin. But after an hour or so my mind would kick back into gear, and the what-ifs would resurface as fearful thoughts. *What if Mum didn't quite understand what I was saying? What if she wasn't really concentrating when I was explaining my worry?* So, I'd go back to her, tug on her sleeve and utter the phrase 'Can I ask you something?', and we would do it all over again. Panic, then relief, then peace, then the bubbles of panic rising once again.

For the first few months, this routine was manageable. I'd form my jumbled thoughts and fears into questions for my mum once or twice a day. But after a while, I was tugging at her sleeve ten to fifteen times a day. The relief that her patient explanations produced lasted for less and less time, and it became no match for my panic and overzealous imagination. I'd go to my mum first thing in the morning, while she was frantically preparing breakfast and school lunches; on our walk to school, when my brother was dawdling far enough behind us not to hear; on our walk back home after school; while Mum was getting dinner ready in our tiny kitchen, which could barely fit two people; and before bed. While I was at school, or anywhere she wasn't present, I'd formulate the questions I'd ask later and commit them to memory, playing them over and over in my head to deal with the constant anxiety I was feeling. My mum would become understandably exasperated at times, but mostly she listened calmly to my ramblings and reassured me gently, knowing full well that I'd be back within the next half hour with the same question, just asked in a slightly different way. The woman was a saint!

Providing constant reassurance to a child, or anyone, with OCD isn't particularly helpful in the long term. However, at this stage no one knew that I had OCD, and this fact wouldn't come out for a very long time. It was the 1990s, an excellent era for boob tubes and camo pants but not so much for nuanced discussions about mental health. I was pestering my mum multiple times a day, but apart from that I was very good at hiding my distress. I did well at school, I had plenty of friends, and I was an excitable, enthusiastic (albeit overly anxious) child. Constant rumination and reassurance-seeking were the only ways I knew to pacify my anguish, and I struggle to think about what I'd have done without my mum's unwavering support. This is why one obsession I developed when I was ten years old was particularly upsetting.

I'd been camping with my Irish friend, Bridget, and her slightly dysfunctional family at a seaside town near Barcelona for ten days. No matter how much time I spent with them, I was always entranced by their strong Northern Irish accents. Linda, Bridget's mum, was a lovely, softly spoken woman who was constantly exasperated by her kids. Bridget was a sharp-tongued tomboy with a habit of getting into punch-ups with her brothers.

Throughout the vacation, I was drowning in homesickness and various obsessions (still mostly on the topic of contracting AIDS). I realised that it probably wasn't an option to bring up the subject with my Irish guardians. 'Hey guys, I think I might have AIDS ... Can someone pass the potatoes?' Without a mobile phone or access to email to contact my mum, my safety net had disappeared, and I retreated into my head for large parts of the trip. I was trying to enjoy the Spanish sun and wash off my worries by splashing around in one of the many pools at the caravan park, but for much of the time I was on autopilot. I was going around in circles in my head, trying to disprove the theory that my brain had established as fact— I had AIDS, and I'd soon pass it on to everyone I loved.

I wanted desperately to move through the world with the same presence that Bridget possessed. It seemed to me that her biggest dilemma throughout the holiday was working out how many different ways she could stitch up her little brother, strategically placing him in Linda's firing line. But I was stuck. After obsessively counting down the days, hours and minutes until I'd be home, the time finally came to leave Spain. I felt enormous relief as I knocked on our apartment door, knowing I'd soon be able to unload my avalanche of worries onto my mum and feel safe once again. But in the excitement of seeing her face and answering her questions about the trip, my mind was hijacked by a barrage of thoughts: *Your mum looks different. This isn't your mum. Something about her has changed . . . maybe this is someone pretending to be your mum?* I know that this sounds very meta and—let's be honest—completely insane. But that didn't make the thoughts any less alarming to me.

My mind had found a way to target the most precious thing in my world and make me question everything I knew to be true. But I couldn't possibly confront this new mystery mum, because if it's someone pretending to be her, she'd just say what I wanted to hear, wouldn't she? My mind became tangled in knots, and I suddenly felt a bottomless despair that I hadn't known before. I tried to think my way out of it, and sank into a depression for a few weeks, which my parents most likely put down to 'tweenage' hormones. Eventually the thoughts subsided, but from that day onwards it felt like my brain had entered a new phase. I no longer knew what was real and what was a trick played by my imagination.

I was losing my sanity.

OCD seems to attack the things that you value the most. For me, when I was still in the pre-teen years, that was my family and my sense of security (and the Spice Girls, but luckily the OCD stayed well clear of that love affair). For so long, my obsessions revolved around my health and the thought of dying a horrible death. But now they were starting to shift again.

We were on a long holiday around Europe and Asia before heading back home to Melbourne for good. There was nothing that excited me more than travelling with my family; the airports, the plane food (I was an easily pleased child), the hotels, the family dinners at restaurants—I found them all exhilarating. But only as long as I felt that everything was 'perfect'. If things didn't feel right, or an unusual or disturbing thought popped into my head, the excitement would be replaced with panic.

On a horse ride on a beach in Cha-am, Thailand, I was struck by another random thought: *What if my dad is gay?* It seems like a strange thought for a ten-year-old, but words such as 'gay' and 'homo' were being thrown around at school, and I was only just starting to learn what they meant. I knew from family conversations that being gay wasn't a bad thing. My godfather was gay, after all. It was never a big deal. But from peers at school in the nineties, I was getting a different message: to be gay was to be 'less than'. I started to wonder if gay people could remain married to someone of the opposite sex. I'd seen photos of my dad dressed up as a woman from his amateur theatre days and I'd also seen a photo of him pretending to kiss his male boss on the cheek. So, what if these things added up to him being gay? He would have to leave my mum, and our family would be broken.

What if my mum didn't know? I'd have to break it to her.

Poor Mum. This conversation wasn't on her 1997 bingo card. I spent the next week on the Gulf of Thailand's pure white shores, divulging to her that I thought her husband was secretly gay. She gently rebuffed my claims, explaining that a fondness for theatre and a playful peck on the cheek weren't evidence of a change in sexual preference. In the same way that I felt a weighty responsibility to keep my parents safe from having a car crash when I was six years old, I now felt responsible for keeping my family together.

I didn't understand it at the time, but I was making invisible connections between things and slowly creating a destructive web of fear. None of these connections was real, but because I'd thought them, they felt real to me. I couldn't bear any level of uncertainty, which I equated to feeling unsafe—and when I felt unsafe, I was fearful.

UN/CERTAINTY

People with OCD can experience so many different variations: contamination fears, suicidal obsessions, questions around their very existence. So what could possibly bind us all together? Uncertainty. Or rather, the quest to achieve absolute, 100 per cent, indubitable certainty.

I didn't realise this until I started to see Dr Andrea Wallace (whom you'll meet again later in the book as the clinical psychologist who diagnosed my OCD). It had never occurred to me that what I'd been doing since I was a little kid was seeking certainty whenever a thought scared me. What I definitely didn't know at the time was that seeking certainty is like searching for the pot of gold at the end of a rainbow: it's a noble but futile quest.

The *feeling* of certainty

In his book *Freedom from Obsessive-Compulsive Disorder*, psychologist Dr Jonathan Grayson talks at length about certainty, and more specifically about our illusion of certainty.[12] We all know what it's like to *feel* certain, but—whether we have OCD or not—what most of us don't realise is that we can never achieve absolute certainty about anything. Ever. We have events that are probable or improbable. That's it.

For those of us with OCD, we experience the illusion of certainty in particular areas of our lives—it could be that when we leave for work, we're sure that our house will still be standing when we return. Or it might be that we're certain the sun will rise in the morning. Because we feel certain about these things, we crave this same feeling when we're anxious about something else—for example, that our newborn baby might not be breathing when we go to bed.

'What most people don't realise is that what they experience as a certainty is not a fact, but a feeling,' writes Dr Grayson.[13] When we try to gain certainty to alleviate our anxiety, we use logic. But, as Dr Grayson points out that, logic won't change our feelings.

A PHILOSOPHICAL DISORDER

When I started writing this book, Dr Jonathan Grayson's name was popping up everywhere: in books, in my therapy sessions and on numerous OCD-related websites. I hunted down his email address and sent a message asking if we could chat at some point. He kindly agreed to speak to me.

An expert in the area of OCD, Dr Grayson has worked with sufferers for over three decades and is Director of the Grayson LA Treatment Center for Anxiety and OCD. He is eminently qualified to discuss the subject of OCD. He also speaks with the confidence you would expect from a white, American, middle-aged professional. But, refreshingly, he sounds genuinely excited when talking about OCD.

'I think OCD is, in some sense, a philosophical disorder,' Dr Grayson begins, when I ask him why he is so fascinated by OCD. 'Most of the concerns that people have are the great questions philosophers ask. "How can I be safe in a world where my family and I could die at any moment? What is the evil in me? What is the nature of God? Who am I?" And the only difference between somebody who has OCD and a great philosopher . . .?' The way he poses the question, I can't tell if it's rhetorical or if he wants an answer.

'There's only one difference,' he continues, before I can speak. 'People with OCD actually want an answer.'

The gun test

Dr Grayson uses something with his clients called the gun test, where he focuses on what they *guess*, not what they *know*. He asks them to imagine that they have a gun pointed at them or a loved one, and when they're asked a question on the topic of their obsession—for example, did they leave the iron on? Have they really contracted AIDS?—they have just one chance to guess the answer. If that guess is wrong, the client or their loved one will be killed. He stresses that the client doesn't have to be confident in their guess, but the idea is to differentiate what they know intellectually and logically from the emotional *feeling* of certainty that they desire.

Dr Grayson points out that, to date, everyone has made the 'right guess': that is, the same guess that people without OCD would make. Their guess probably won't *feel* right—but it's a good reminder that this feeling doesn't really matter. Learning to live with uncertainty needs to be one of the goals of the person with OCD—and this is where exposure and response prevention (ERP) comes into play.

Better than normal

I ask Dr Grayson if those of us with OCD can ever get comfortable with uncertainty when we've been fearful of it for so long.

'Research has shown us that the only people who are certain are stupid. And people with OCD tend to be above average intelligence, so they can't be dumb enough to be certain,' he says. I won't argue with that!

Dr Grayson is revving up now. It's obvious that uncertainty is his thing. 'When you overcome your OCD, you're not going to be normal—you're going to be *better* than normal, because the average person does not cope well with uncertainty. They may be coping better than you right now, but they don't really cope with it. They're really good at denial. You don't get to do denial. You get heaven or hell. I think you've done an excellent study of hell. Let's try the other,' he says, gesturing wildly with his hands.

'Study of hell' is probably the best description of OCD I've ever heard. I like this man, and I love his passion.

The odds

'Do you know what saves your children?' It's another Dr Grayson question that sounds rhetorical, but I soon realise he's waiting for an answer. 'Luck,' he continues, putting me out of my misery. 'The odds are they won't be kidnapped. The odds are they won't die of a dreaded disease. The odds are they won't fall down the stairs and crack their head open. But it does happen. So, all you have is the odds.'

I don't know about you, but hearing that made my heart beat faster and my palms sweat. I can't rely on *odds* to keep my children alive. I failed Probability in Year 12! My kids are still alive because I watch them like a hawk! But then I remember a horrendous experience I had with my eldest son a few days earlier, when he came bolting up the stairs, red-faced, pointing at his throat. He had swallowed a $2 coin and couldn't breathe. I was desperately fumbling with my phone to call an ambulance, terror and panic coursing through my body, when he started vomiting. I heard the *ping* of a coin bounce on the marble floor—the most beautiful sound I've ever heard. I know that I can't watch my kids all the time, but the dice rolled the right way that day; the coin didn't lodge in his throat. My five-year-old was saved by the odds.

I tell Dr Grayson this story and he nods, expressing sympathy for my experience of parental terror. His advice? Don't push that feeling of terror away. Embrace it.

I'd rather push it way down to the depths of my soul, where it will never again see the light of day. When I ask him why I should embrace it, he mounts a case that's hard to argue against.

'Because it's a real feeling that you have. For you to say, "I'm going to push that away because that's too icky to think about", that doesn't work. So, learn to cope with the feeling. And what do you get when you surrender? Well, then the present begins to mean something. The only time you have your family is when you're with them; the rest of the time, they're nice memories. But if you're in the middle of OCD, you don't even have that. You're in OCD land.'

WHO GETS OCD AND WHY?

It's thought that OCD is both biological and learned; there are genetic, neurological and environmental factors that may increase the risk for OCD. Twin and family studies show that genetics play a role in the development of OCD, but, to date, data has come from small studies and larger scale research is needed for conclusive results.[14]

While writing this book, there has been growing excitement about a new study by a prominent Australian medical research institute, QIMR Berghofer, which offers more insight into the neurobiology of OCD. The 2023 study has confirmed that it's likely OCD sufferers experience an imbalance in particular signalling pathways within the brain, linked to emotional regulation and reward. The researchers stress that they are not the first group to make this finding, but the fact that these findings have been replicated means that more targeted treatments can start to be developed.[15]

In his book, Dr Jonathan Grayson talks about OCD being a neurobiological disorder that results in a chemical imbalance in the brain. He explains that because of the unavailability of serotonin in specific parts of the brain, those with OCD are more likely to respond to uncertainty with discomfort, and less likely to respond to task completion with satisfaction.[16]

'For OCD, the threshold for those two things is less. It takes less uncertainty for you to feel more anxious, and when you complete something, you don't get the feeling, which drives people with OCD crazy. You end up in that state of, "I know I did this, but why don't I know I did this?"' explains Dr Grayson during our chat.

'But, as almost every sufferer knows, it's not every uncertainty that gets you,' he continues.

The learned component of OCD involves classical and operant conditioning. I'm not going to get into the details of these; however, in a nutshell, classical conditioning relates to the process through which feelings come to be associated with situations or thoughts that were previously either neutral or associated with a different feeling; and operant conditioning refers to the process through which you learn to engage in behaviours to avoid aversive feelings (such as anxiety) and to attain positive feelings (such as certainty).[17]

THE 'BIG BANG' OF THE OCD 'UNIVERSE'

You know that feeling when you have a sudden realisation that makes your stomach leap and your hair stand on end? Maybe you forgot to pick up your kid from school. Or perhaps you accidentally sent a message to your boss, calling them a fuckwit, instead of to your best friend. It's that moment of panic when all the terrifying consequences of your actions flood your brain, and your body activates the ancient fight, flight or freeze response that dates back to the time when sabre-toothed tigers stalked cavemen. The fight, flight or freeze response has resulted in an ability we still have today—which has most likely been useful at some point—to get yourself out of trouble.

However, for people with OCD, this survival response can be triggered by an intrusive thought that is, more often than not, irrational and unlikely. We have received a threat, and we will then find something to 'do' to make this uncomfortable feeling go away (the compulsion).

Clinical psychologist Dr David J. Keuler has written a fascinating article about how understanding the first few moments of an OCD obsession can give us a vital insight into how to beat it. He suggests that just as astrophysicists study the Big Bang theory to decode the mysteries of the universe, the OCD 'universe' can be understood in a similar way. 'What begins as a small hot spot of discomfort expands into a complex galaxy of obsessions and compulsions,' he writes.[18]

No one really knows why a certain thought takes hold and turns into an obsession, at the particular time it takes place.

I vividly remember the moment I noticed a faint splash of blood on the seat that I'd just been sitting on and suddenly remembered the news story I'd seen about a man dying of AIDS and learning that it can be transmitted through contact with infected blood; for me, this is the moment my AIDS obsession took hold. The fears that were suddenly flooding me felt too heavy and dangerous, so I started to do things such as avoid public toilets, seek reassurance from my mum and, for many years, hover over any toilet seat, ending up in an awkward squat position (on the bright side, I got very toned quads). This was my OCD 'universe' beginning to reveal itself. I labelled an uncomfortable thought as unwanted; a survival response was activated; and, in turn, a behaviour response followed. This paved the pathway that I'd go down every single time a similar thought appeared in my brain.

Dr Keuler explains that in a conventional universe—that is, in the brain of someone without OCD—intrusive thoughts, physical sensations and emotions can float freely around each other without exerting a gravitational pull on any compulsive behaviours. 'Compulsions, avoidance and paralysis maintain obsessions in awareness by providing the necessary gravitational pull to hold the whole system together. Remove that gravity, and the system unravels.'[19]

David Adam, who wrote the brilliant book *The Man Who Couldn't Stop*, vividly remembers when his OCD 'universe' exploded into existence (his fears were also about contracting AIDS). 'My OCD began with an intrusive thought, a snow-flake that fell from the summer sky,' he writes poetically. He'd suddenly remembered a conversation he'd had with a friend following a one-night stand with a girl at college. The throw-away line, 'You could have AIDS', hastily re-entered his consciousness, where it would remain, tormenting him, for years to come. To nullify the pain that the thought caused him, he would repeatedly ring the National Aids Hotline to receive reassurance that he didn't have AIDS, or he would donate blood so they could test it and tell him he was fine. However, none of his compulsions resulted in long-lasting relief.[20]

In order to disrupt this whole sequence of events, Dr Keuler suggests using mindfulness to try to resist the fight, flight or freeze response and the labelling of the thought, feeling or sensation. He says to look at the situation with the interest and detachment of a scientist, and try to resist the urge to perform a compulsion (you'll learn more about resisting compulsions using ERP in Chapter 8). Disrupting the immediate sequence of events upon OCD's arrival, Dr Keuler suggests, will help to steer the sufferer out of the OCD 'universe' and into a more peaceful place. However, he admits that this is much easier said than done.[21] But it's an interesting concept: looking at how OCD began, to gain a better understanding of how to overcome it.

Chapter 2

THE PEAK

I have this vivid memory of my first 'casual clothes day' at high school. It was only a couple of months into my first year at a co-ed private school that sits arrogantly among the leafy streets of Kew. I tortured myself for days over what to wear, because high school was turning out to be the judgemental, competitive jungle that all the American rom-coms I watched promised it would be. I settled on some low-rise Levi jeans with pink stitching, and a cropped mint-coloured top from KOOKAÏ. I loved fashion, but I was still a daggy, innocent tween who watched *Spice World* on VHS more times than I care to admit.

I wasn't trying to dress in a sexy way or draw attention to myself, but the entire day I had comments about how the jeans

I wore 'showed off my arse' and flat stomach. The observations flying around were mainly coming from boys, and they weren't necessarily derogatory, but I was suddenly hyper-aware of my body in a way that I never had been before. I quickly learned that to be accepted in this bubble of brutal social hierarchy, you must shave your legs, at least 'pretend' you've given a blow job and, for fuck's sake, TAKE A JOKE! My friend's boyfriend gave her the nickname 'thunder thighs'. Her *boyfriend*. When any of us objected to any of these kinds of 'jokes', we were told we were too uptight.

For the most part I actually enjoyed high school, but it felt like I went from being an innocent teeny-bopper in Year 6 to a self-conscious young woman in a matter of minutes. The sudden sexualisation that I—and I'm sure many others—experienced in high school was harsh and confusing for me. I started to obsess about turning into a sexual deviant. I had innocent crushes on boys and was interested in 'dating', but all I felt comfortable doing was holding hands and repeatedly tracing their name in my school diary. However, my head was suddenly full of sexually explicit images, and I was terrified that I'd do something which would brand me with a label that I could never escape.

Girls and women were (and still are) expected to walk an absurd tightrope between being 'too frigid' and 'too slutty'. As I've gotten older, I've tried to reject this Madonna–whore dichotomy. But at the time, it seemed to be an unquestionable reality. Be *good* but not *boring*. Be *girly* but don't be *like other girls*. I became so concerned that if I had a boyfriend I'd end up going 'too far' with them, I just kept my distance and tried to separate myself from the 'cool' crowd, who would go to parties and drink in the park. Because whenever certain images and situations scared me, I immediately jumped to the conclusion that they would eventuate. Maybe I'd give some guy a hand job under the table? Maybe I'd have sex in a cupboard at a party? I didn't trust myself. So, I avoided any potential situation that could lead to something bad happening. Instead, I focused on studying and spending time with friends who were still more interested in going to the movies than going down on guys.

The first time I met Dan was at a restaurant in Williamstown when I was in Year 10. We were both studying French, and the teacher had organised a special excursion to a French restaurant so we could practise ordering *pommes frites* and *escargots* with a waiter called Bill from Altona North. I'd never spoken to Dan before, as he was in the year above me. He was as comfortable conjugating French verbs as he was barrelling a footy across an oval. He was also extremely kind, so he may as well have been a magical unicorn.

I found myself sitting opposite him at the restaurant table, and it wasn't long before we were chatting and placing bets on who could eat the most snails without dry-retching. He had a supreme confidence that made him seem like he was floating just slightly above everyone else. It was the kind of confidence that can only come from being a decorated athlete at an elite private school AND having a brain. As an introvert who had always wanted to be an extrovert, I was drawn to and fascinated by him. We were two extremely naive kids and, unbeknown to us, we were about to hop on a relationship rollercoaster that would clumsily stop and start for the next ten years.

Because I was so worried about being labelled a slut, and seeing as though no couple could have a sexual experience that wasn't then proclaimed to the entire school by a town crier, I was very clear about 'going slow' with Dan for the first couple of months of our relationship. But as soon as we started to become sexually active, I began to obsess about whether I was pregnant. It was literally impossible, because we hadn't had penetrative sex, but facts never get in the way of a good obsession! It wasn't as if I didn't understand how the mechanics of reproduction worked. I did. I'd even pinged myself in the eye with a condom in Year 6 Sex Ed, when we were told to practise putting condoms on bananas. But logic didn't have any traction.

If I was being sexually active in any capacity, then *maybe* some semen had found its way into my uterus? The risk was small—microscopic, in fact—but the potential fallout seemed too great. For months I was so fearful of becoming a teen mum who would have to somehow fit my school dress over a baby bump that I bought dozens of pregnancy tests and would only feel any sense of fleeting calm once I saw the single line show up on the white, plastic stick. I now recognise, after years of therapy, that these fears were more about my identity—and shame associated with sexual behaviour—than pregnancy itself.

However, at the time I was just worrying about the fear that was dangling in front of me, no matter how insane it seemed.

Eventually this fear of being pregnant disappeared. But in a classic obsessive-compulsive disorder (OCD) move, it only disappeared because it was replaced with another fear: that I was gay. Now, I want to make it very clear that I don't believe there's *anything* shameful about being gay. Even though, at the time, words such as 'gay', 'homo' and 'dyke' were still being savagely flung around the schoolyard, I knew in my core that it wasn't bad to be gay. I grew up in a progressive household that never questioned different ways of being in this world. It wasn't so much the being gay that scared me, it was the thought that perhaps I had no control over who I was, or who I was going to be with. I was truly happy in my relationship, and the thought of having to end it scared me.

I remember being on holidays and mindlessly flicking through the TV channels.

'Cricket . . . no, tennis . . . no, loud lesbian sex . . . what?' I'm still unsure how I landed on lesbian porn on free-to-air TV during the day, but that's beside the point. Because of my long-held worry about contracting AIDS, as well as my obsession around pregnancy, anything sex-related generally filled me with anxiety. Suddenly being confronted by two naked women passionately making love made me slightly anxious but also a bit curious. I watched it for a while, a little confused as to why I was finding it so erotic. But, seeing as though I wasn't the only one in the house, I quickly clicked back to Richie Benaud claiming something was 'marvellous' from the commentators' box at the Sydney Cricket Ground. I went about my own business until a thought thrust itself into my head so unexpectedly, I almost fell over: *You must be a lesbian.*

Wait what? No. Nah, I don't think so.

Am I?

And again, just like when I first experienced the thoughts about having AIDS, I remembered playing 'mums and dads' as a young kid, with other girls. So, I must be gay. Case closed. Knowing what I do now, after years of therapy, it's obvious that I was experiencing thought-action fusion (TAF). This is when you have a thought and immediately believe that just having the thought is equivalent to carrying out the action. Because I had the thought that *maybe I'm a lesbian*, I skipped 100 steps ahead and believed it was inevitable.

In the first few moments of this burgeoning obsession, I started to experience the fight, flight or freeze response: I tried to 'think' my way out of the thought (fight), I judged my inner experience as 'bad' or 'unwanted' (flight), and my body was tense and anxious (freeze). As had happened multiple times before in my young life, I soon began to develop behaviours in response to this intimidating thought. Behaviours that would dictate my life, steal my presence and threaten my sanity. One of the devastating things about OCD is that it makes you believe that you don't have any agency in your life. You can't make decisions; they're made for you, and you just need to follow the path unfolding in front of you, whether you like it or not. And more often than not with OCD, the path is leading somewhere that you don't want to go.

Most people's teenage years are pretty fraught. I'm very aware that, compared to many people, I was extremely lucky. I had a loving family, close friends and a privileged life. However, having sexually themed OCD obsessions during a time of sexual discoveries and experimentation was particularly over-whelming and disorientating. Anyone who's ever been to high school knows that most things tend to revolve around sex to some degree. *Who do you have a crush on? Who did you pash on camp? Who had a threesome at the formal afterparty?* Testosterone, progesterone and oestrogen fly around madly like seagulls at a beach barbecue.

Any time a thought about being gay popped into my head, instead of noticing it and moving on, I'd try to disprove the theory to myself. If I was watching a film and there was a scene with two girls kissing, I'd usually have to spend hours thinking about why I *wouldn't* actually want to do that in real life. I'd replay the scene in my head, but insert myself as a character, trying to work out what sorts of feelings I'd get *if* that was me. Or I'd rewatch the film repeatedly, checking how my body reacted each time. You can imagine how tedious and exhausting this is. You end up tying yourself in knots, because your mind can imagine anything. Confirmation bias comes into play, with your mind focusing solely on the information that supports the hypothesis you've already established. Because I was spending a lot of spare time with people—friends, boyfriend, family—I'd often have to remove myself from social situations so that I could perform these mental compulsions and try to make sense of the thoughts flying around my brain. Once I felt that temporary sense of completion that Dr Jonathan Grayson mentions, described in the previous chapter, I could re-join the world. (This is when I started to linger in toilet cubicles again.) Rumours about my bathroom dawdles were no doubt swirling about, but I didn't have the brain space to think or care about that.

Of course, thinking my way out of fundamental questions about my identity and future were fruitless. Occasionally, I'd reach an agreement with my brain and feel a few minutes or perhaps even an hour of relief. But as I now understand, performing any kind of compulsion will only reinforce the obsession, guaranteeing that it will eventually rise back to the surface with even greater force.

These thinking compulsions would occur all the time throughout my late teens and early twenties: when I was in class, when I was having a conversation with a friend or when I was having sex. Any time. Any place. Other compulsions included having long showers—particularly after sex—during which I'd try to think my way out of my obsessions, and avoiding any TV shows or movies that might have any kind of sex scene. I was either stuck in the past (did I think/feel that?) or in the future (would I enjoy this?), so I was rarely in the present moment. It was torturous. But like so many others with OCD, I desperately wanted to portray an image of 'competence'. Throwing up my arms and conceding defeat (which is how I saw it then, not now) by admitting that I wasn't coping was almost scarier than my thoughts.

Quite often I'd still go to my mum for reassurance. 'Hey Mum, if I have this thought, does it make me gay?' 'Hey Mum, if I was giving head and I felt my gag reflex, does that mean I'm not into guys?' MY POOR MUM. I know most parents want their teenagers to feel comfortable enough to come to them with *any* question, but this was pushing the envelope. And sometimes my brain would play sick games with me. The more R-rated the thought, the more insistent my mind was that I needed to get reassurance from my mum. HOW WILL YOU KNOW IF YOU DON'T ASK HER? I was so worried that if I didn't know this particular thing about myself *for certain*, then I didn't know myself at all. It was hell. Talking in graphic detail about sex-related things with a parent once or twice is uncomfortable. But I'd go through periods when it was every day. Multiple times a day. Sometimes, multiple times *an hour*. It was mortifying. But the alternative was more agonising, which hopefully conveys just how harrowing it is to have OCD.

Mum was actively encouraging me to talk to a counsellor or psychologist by this stage, but I emphatically refused. I had absolutely no idea that what I was experiencing—and had been experiencing since I was a child—was OCD. I knew a bit about anxiety and thought perhaps I had that, but in my naive mind I believed that people who sought help for their mental state were *crazy*. I didn't want to be seen as crazy. And so I was living a double life: on the outside I tried to project the image of a capable, successful, social, smart young woman, but on the inside it was an incessant cacophony of fears, what-ifs and doubts. This kind of exertion always takes its toll; early in my final year of high school, my body and mind capitulated under the intense pressure.

I was one of those students who tried to do everything: music, sport, volunteering. I also desperately wanted to get a perfect score in the exams at the end of the year. The thoughts would bubble up throughout my days, but because I was so busy—usually rowing on the Yarra River by 5 a.m. and finishing other extracurricular activities well after 5 p.m.—my ruminations would grab hold at night-time. It got to the point where I just wasn't sleeping. I couldn't turn the noise down. But then I'd get up and do it all again the next day. Until I couldn't.

At the beginning of my final year of school, I was diagnosed with glandular fever. After months of little sleep, my body decided that sleep is all it would do. I was completely devoid of energy, which fortunately gave my mind a brief break from the endless whirlpool of obsessions.

Throughout the turbulence of my late adolescence, Dan and I were still dating, and I was still in an eternal war against my thoughts. I hadn't really explained any of my chaotic inner battles to Dan, mainly because I had no idea where to begin. I had no understanding of what was going on, so how could I find the language to package it up nicely for someone else? I couldn't. It was impossible. So, I tried to paint over the cracks and hoped he wouldn't notice.

I made it to the end of the school year, limping to the finish line. I managed to get through my final exams and while I didn't get a perfect score, I did very well and was accepted into a Media and Communications degree. I had no concrete ideas about what I'd do next, but I had a high score and was heading to a prestigious university, and these were the things that we were taught to aim for at school. These were the markers of success. So, I'd keep going in that direction. Work hard, do well and project an image of 'achieving'.

Not long after finishing school, I decided to get my nose pierced. I did it and loved it. The next day, on a break from my shift at Surf Dive 'n Ski at Melbourne Central shopping centre, I read an article about *American Idol* winner Kelly Clarkson that featured an unverified rumour about her being into women. Looking at the photo accompanying the article, I noticed that she had a nose ring. It was on the same side as mine. I started to google images of other women with nose rings, and noticed that they were all on the opposite side. But I got mine on the same side as Kelly's? And it seems like she's gay? The next day, I went back to the piercing salon to get my nose pierced on the opposite side. I realise how unhinged this sounds, and I'm cringing as I write about it. But this is the point that I'd reached. While my obsessions at the time were still underpinned by a theme of sexual identity, there was no real rhyme or reason to my thoughts and compulsions. None of it was making sense. I was just having a thought and then reacting in an often irrational or erratic way.

A soft, wise voice in my head was telling me, *Stop. Take a minute. Investigate the madness in your brain*. But by performing compulsions in response to my obsessions, I had the illusion of control. If I kicked this can down the road for long enough, then maybe it would disappear, and I could wash my hands of all this nonsense. Life could start anew, and I could finally be at peace . . . without having to face any uncomfortable truths.

WHY DO WE WORRY ABOUT CERTAIN THINGS?

I won't spend much time on this, because I don't want to give the impression that the particular OCD themes really *matter*. The actual content of the obsessions isn't important. It's how someone with OCD reacts to them—with fear, misery, dread or anxiety—that matters. However, questions often arise about why certain themes tend to stick around, or why they morph throughout different life stages.

Clinical psychologist Dr Andrea Wallace says that we tend to have underlying belief systems that may affect what we worry about most. For some, it could be an overdeveloped sense of responsibility for keeping people safe, which might result in Harm OCD, or it might be an overestimation of risk, which could cause someone to worry about contamination.

She says that a good therapist will work towards figuring out what the *underlying fear* is behind the specific intrusive thoughts. If someone, for example, is terrified by the thought that they might molest their baby, she says that an underlying fear could be that their partner might leave them because they are a 'bad' person.

'The compulsive behaviour becomes getting reassurance from their partner that the thought is permissible and that their partner still sees them as a good person. Like the terror is actually, "Am I unlovable to the people who love me?"' Dr Wallace explains.

It's common for OCD to peak around times of significant change or upheaval: high-school exams, moving away from home, starting a new job, getting married or having kids. These big life events always come with uncertainty, and this can set off fireworks in the brain of someone with OCD.

People with OCD tend to care very deeply about other people, and they often have a feeling of over-responsibility—for other people, things and situations. OCD latches on to the things that are most important to us, and these things, understandably, tend to change over time. However, for some people, the themes can stay the same, or they may return after years of dormancy. The important point is that all OCD themes are treatable, and none is 'better' or 'worse' than any other one.

WHY IS OCD SO MISUNDERSTOOD?

We only have to look at how people with OCD have histori-cally been portrayed in movies to answer this question, such as Melvin Udall in *As Good As it Gets*, a narcissist who displayed Contamination and Magical Thinking OCD themes; Howard Hughes in *The Aviator*, an unstable and eccentric businessman who was terrified of germs; and Roy Waller in *Matchstick Men*, a miserable and irritable con man who couldn't open a door or window without counting to three. I'm not suggesting that these portrayals of OCD are entirely wrong, but the protagonists are all unlikeable, volatile (male) germaphobes. Growing up, I never once considered that I had OCD, largely because of what I thought I knew about the disorder from TV and film.

Like so many other mental disorders, OCD is a complex illness that can present and be experienced in many ways. But for so long it's been trivialised and distilled to become something more digestible to audiences, and exaggerated in the media to the point of mockery. For months, my local cafe had a sign saying: 'We have OCD: Obsessive Coffee Disorder'.

A RE-EDUCATION

So, why would people announce publicly that they have OCD—and try to correct the narrative—if their daily hell is laughed at, mocked and minimised? When I ask social worker and OCD therapist Elizabeth McIngvale about this, she says that it's become much more complicated than just educating the public about OCD.

'I think that, unfortunately for us, not only do we have to educate [other people about] what it is, we have to re-educate [them about] what it's *not*. It's almost like breaking a habit versus just learning something for the first time. It's easier to do one or the other,' she says.

McIngvale is a pretty striking antidote to the OCD movie characters of the 1990s and early 2000s. An impeccably well-dressed woman in her thirties with impossibly white teeth and flowing blonde locks, she has turned her OCD nightmare as a teenager into motivation to help countless others. She experienced such severe Contamination OCD when she was fifteen that she would have extensive shower routines that would last for hours and was unable to dress herself for fear of something bad happening. After finally receiving the right treatment, she became the first public advocate for the International OCD Foundation (IOCDF) and is now the Director of the OCD Institute of Texas.

While she was keen to help others so they wouldn't experience the same difficulties she did in getting help, it wasn't always easy being so public about her illness.

'I was dating someone once and they'd watched one of my videos and one day they were being weird and awkward. They made a comment like, "Yeah, but I can't believe you would *do* that." And I was like, "What? I would never do that." They had watched a video where I opened up about my sexual intrusive thoughts and, in turn, they thought I would act on them. I think that because of the taboo nature of OCD, it's easy to just be like, "That is so weird" and label someone. It is so important to know that our thoughts scare us and we hate them—we are not them and don't want to engage in them,' she explains.

Thanks to McIngvale's courage, there are now dozens of IOCDF advocates, and luckily we now see more varied depictions of OCD in the media. However, there's still a long way to go to ensure that OCD is more widely understood as a serious mental illness, instead of just a quirky annoyance.

'PURE O'

While some kinds of OCD will drive the sufferer to perform physical compulsions such as repeating words, cleaning or checking, others will result in more mental compulsions such as reviewing thoughts or feelings, constantly replaying situations in the mind, or avoiding situations that might trigger unwanted feelings, thoughts or urges. Purely obsessional OCD (aka 'Pure O') isn't a clinical term, but it's widely used to describe the various subtypes of OCD that often don't have outwardly obvious compulsions (for example, Harm OCD, Sexual Orientation OCD, Relationship OCD, Trans OCD and Paedophilia OCD).

Some clinicians push back against the name 'Pure O', because it suggests that people suffering it don't perform compulsions. They absolutely do, but the behavioural component of the illness is more subtle to the outside world. The motivation behind the mental compulsions is the same as for physical compulsions—to eradicate the anxiety that thoughts are causing. Thoughts that tend to torture those with 'Pure O' are generally discordant with their *actual* values and desires.

A tip for dealing with dark intrusive thoughts

When I began exposure and response prevention (ERP) I found that I was always being tripped up whenever I was trying to 'accept' horrific thoughts. If, for example, you get caught up in an obsession about contracting an illness, the idea with ERP is to accept the uncertainty and say something to yourself like 'Maybe I will get sick. The chances are that I won't, but there is a chance that I will.' It's not an easy thing to accept, but there is little shame or taboo in it. However, I could never say to myself, 'Yeah cool, maybe I am a paedophile.' It's not a topic that I could introduce ambiguity into and feel remotely okay about.

When I asked Dr Wallace about this, she empathised with this conundrum and told me to instead say something to myself like 'I'm having *the thought* that I'm a paedophile right now, and it's really hard to have this thought.' Clearly separating the thought from myself allows me the space to contextualise these awful experiences. I am not my thoughts, and my thoughts are not me. This is an example of cognitive diffusion and you can find more information about this in Chapter 11.

SUFFERING IN SILENCE

Obsessions that can plague someone experiencing 'Pure O' are often tangled with distressing and dark topics such as violence (towards others or yourself) or paedophilia. These are tough topics to think about, let alone talk about, which is why many people with OCD suffer in silence—they fear that others will believe that these thoughts represent their *actual* desires.

But it's important to shine a light on these obsessions and make it very clear that people with OCD are suffering *because* they find the content of these thoughts so distressing. These are good people who are being tortured by dark thoughts. While most people will experience intrusive thoughts about all kinds of issues, people with OCD will tend to react to these thoughts with sheer terror; this strong emotional response to merely thinking something means that the thoughts are much more likely to recur.

Dr Andrea Wallace works with numerous clients who are tormented by intrusive thoughts about taboo subjects. She finds that society at large does a poor job of distinguishing between thoughts and actions, which she suggests is incredibly problematic for people with OCD.

'A person will often say, "Well, just having the thought means you are a paedophile." And I say, "No, no, no, that's *not* correct." It's a thought. It's a feeling. It's an image. It's a sensation. These are not behaviours. And they are a *world apart*. All of the feelings, all of the urges, all of the sensations—all of those are innocent, no matter what they are,' Dr Wallace says.

She gives an everyday example to explain further. If we're driving and we're rudely cut off by someone, we generally wouldn't be too distressed by having a sudden urge to punch that person. We know that if push came to shove, we would probably just mutter a swear word under our breath and walk

Ego-syntonic vs ego-dystonic thoughts

Ego-syntonic thoughts are ones that are in line with our values and desires, whereas ego-dystonic thoughts are contrary to our core beliefs. For example, I could have an ego-syntonic worry that I could be kicked out of my rental property, and have nowhere to live. Obviously, I need somewhere stable to live, and would be terrified if I was left homeless. As David Adam explains in *The Man Who Couldn't Stop*, 'thoughts like that are in step with the rules and rhythms of our life ... ego-syntonic thoughts can make us unhappy, but when they do it is their contents and not the thoughts themselves that are the problem. We do not question why we have them.'[1] If I started worrying about this excessively, it could become a symptom of generalised anxiety disorder (GAD).

Ego-dystonic thoughts tend to be more irrational and are completely out of line with how we see ourselves, and want others to see us. When I was living in a fifth-floor apartment building, I used to worry that if I went out on the balcony, I'd jump off it. This was ego-dystonic, and caused me a huge amount of distress, because I knew in my core that I didn't want to kill myself or cause myself injury. And because I labelled this intrusive thought as bad or dangerous, I started to obsess that it was something I wanted, and would do.

off. We most likely wouldn't take a swing at them. But when it comes to thoughts around vulnerable people such as kids, or some kind of sexually deviant behaviour, it terrifies people.

Dr Wallace explains, 'I want people to know that your thoughts, your feelings, your urges, your sensations—they can't make you bad. You can't think the wrong ones. You can't have the wrong urge. But we can absolutely *do* the wrong thing. Paedophilic behaviour is *absolutely* wrong. And I'm not backing down on that. But anything that goes on inside your body is innocent. And there's no ifs and buts about that. Because I think there's a lot more people who are experiencing OCD with concerns like inappropriate sexual behaviour than are letting on. And they are suffering in silence.'

Martin's story

'It's with you every single moment of every single day. Even when you sleep. I have OCD in my dreams.'[2]

This is a quote from Martin Ingle, when he appeared on an episode of ABC TV's *You Can't Ask That* in 2021. The episode was dedicated to busting stereotypical myths about OCD, and Martin was one of the participants talking candidly about his experiences.

I had complicated feelings after watching this episode. I felt so in awe of the people telling their stories. However, it seemed that many of the participants were still sparring with their OCD. They were commentating from inside the ring, telling us in real time about the punches they're dodging and the swings they're throwing, which was both uncomfortable and admirable.

From watching the show, it was obvious to me that Martin had been in front of the camera before. On his website, his bio reads: 'Writer, filmmaker, obsessive compulsive'. When I first speak to Martin over a Zoom call, he is engaging, funny and painfully honest. But I see the same subtle weariness that I observed on the TV screen. A weariness that I very much recognised as coming from years of torment. From being broken into pieces and having to put yourself back together again. From believing the worst about yourself for so long.

Martin was in his twenties when he first experienced an obsession. It started with a fundamental question about his identity. There are addiction issues in his family, so he started to wonder if he was an alcoholic. He had only ever been drunk a handful of times, but he began to question whether it was an unchangeable part of his personality. Over a period of months, the thoughts took a much darker turn. What if he secretly liked the taste of human flesh? This thought had no connection to the previous obsession about being an alcoholic, but with OCD, the themes can change as quickly as the wind.

Martin, who was studying filmmaking and living in a shared house before OCD crept up on him, desperately wanted things to go back to the way they were before this nightmare set in.

'I was just kind of confused and totally overwhelmed by how sudden and how extreme all of these things were. It was unlike anything I'd ever experienced before. And it was not going away. The thoughts presented themselves as problems to be solved—questions about my identity that I could figure out if I just thought *hard enough*. Because that's how I'd solved every problem in my life until then—I had no reason to believe this couldn't be solved, either,' he explains.

Unexpectedly, the thoughts suddenly found fertile ground in various sexual obsessions. While answering my questions, Martin is (understandably) uncomfortable when talking about these themes. He obliges, however, because he wishes that he had read about these kinds of experiences when he was at his worst.

'I started to consider the possibility that I was secretly a sexual pervert. So secretly that I didn't even know. Someone who was sexually aroused by horrible things like animals or family members or children. I mean why not? If the cannibal thing is possible, why not this? This all disgusted me and terrified me, but the doubt didn't stop,' he says.

This is the sort of honesty and courage that should be wholeheartedly applauded. I feel an enormous amount of gratitude to him, and for him.

'I was just trying to figure out if I was fundamentally broken. I was terrified to find out, but you can't stop because you have a moral obligation, because it matters so much to you. It's like a perfect problem.'

I can relate to this idea of a 'perfect problem'. Most of the things OCD sufferers worry about don't have a definitive answer. They're often unsolvable problems that will have you fruitlessly clutching for answers that don't exist.

He started to worry about spreading contaminants from his genitals to unsuspecting people. If he was going to the toilet, for example, and some urine splashed on the floor of his bathroom, he would then have to ensure that every drop was cleaned up before his housemate, who was about to go for a run, used the bathroom. As he explained on *You Can't Ask That*, he was worried that his 'dick germs would be non-consensually spread around the park!'[3]

It got to the point where Martin was terrified of touching his own genitals, for fear of spreading contaminants to others. He rarely had sex and didn't allow himself to masturbate for six years. He is at pains to explain that it wasn't a health-related fear, but more a fundamental question about identity and morality.

Seeking help

Like many others, Martin cycled through a handful of psychologists who didn't identify him as having OCD; each experience was both exhausting and confusing.

'I was terrified; I didn't know what to say. I didn't know how to say it. How do you describe these doubts that you are experiencing? You don't even have the insight or the tools to call them "thoughts", because you're not aware that they're separate to you. When you go through treatment for OCD, you learn how to speak about it, but when you don't know what it is, you can't. You don't go to a psychologist and say, "I'm having intrusive thoughts." So, what do you say? You go to a psychologist and say, "I'm dangerous." Which of course is a terrifying thing to say. And if you're a clueless thera- pist, a terrifying thing to hear, I'm sure,' says Martin.

Martin eventually came across an article about 'Pure O' on the internet and found a clinician who specialised in OCD.

'I said, "This is what I think I have." And she's like, "Yeah, of course. That's exactly what it is." But *I* had to do that. *I* had to figure that out. The whole process took almost a year. And that's not that long, compared to how long it is for a lot of people,' he explains.

When I ask him if it was a relief to get an official OCD diagnosis, he pauses for a long moment before answering.

'I wish I could say that there was one moment where the birds were singing and everything. It . . . it just wasn't like that for me. Because even when you get diagnosed, OCD has a way of still making you doubt whether you have OCD. Even after many years. So, I didn't feel much relief, because the doubt was still there. But at least I had ammunition against it, I had medical professionals on my side.'

While Martin found therapy—particularly exposure and response prevention (ERP)—helpful, his physical compulsions around contami- nation were worsening, to the point where he was worried about eating. He saw a psychiatrist and started medication.

'I'd always thought that it was like a painkiller or a drug, where you take it and then twenty minutes later it would start to work and [you] feel it, you know? But that's not what it was at all. It was much more subtle. I just started to get a little bit clearer. It felt like a weight was very, very slowly being lifted, or at least the pressure was being taken off just a bit. So that I could then do the behaviour therapy.'

Inpatient woes

Almost a year after our first conversation, I call Martin again for an update. He had mentioned in our first talk that he was on the waiting list to get into The Melbourne Clinic's three-week inpatient OCD program, and when I discover that he had completed the course a few months prior, I'm keen to find out how it went. I'm hopeful that completing the only intensive inpatient OCD program in Australia has helped to fast-track his recovery.

This time we don't use the camera on Zoom, so I don't see that same weariness in his face. But I hear it immediately in his voice.

'It was full-on. I suppose it's something I've been almost dreading doing for many years, maybe at first because I thought it was impossible. I was scared of what I might have to do. But then once I realised what exposure therapy actually was, and the fear went away, I still put it off—because I knew it was going to be unpleasant,' he explains.

Martin tells me about the day-to-day activities, and about the difficulty of seeking out exposures, rather than waiting for them to happen incidentally. Much of the day involved doing exposures within a group environment, but they were done incrementally, so as not to overwhelm the participants. They would also be encouraged to do exposures on their own.

'I would do things like go out in public into a coffee shop and, say, be swiping on Tinder or talking to a match on Tinder, which I didn't like to do in public, because there are people around and it felt really wrong to be doing something sexually pleasurable in public. So, basically just finding ways to mess with the system that OCD has built.

'Also, I have trouble making my bed for a bunch of reasons—contamination reasons and intrusive thoughts that I get while making my bed—and so that would be an exposure for me . . . making my bed and essentially, no matter what you do, just sitting with the discomfort,' he says.

There's an edge in Martin's voice that makes me think that the program wasn't as healing as he expected. When I ask him how he found the experience of meeting and working alongside other people with OCD, he takes a deep breath before he responds.

'I had mixed feelings about it . . . I was really looking forward to getting to know people who were like me, and sharing our fears and obsessions and bouncing ideas around and all of that. The frustration I had was that we were encouraged to actually not do that.'

He understands the reason this isn't encouraged (the medical professionals who run the course want to avoid the participants using each other for reassurance-seeking). But he feels that this prevented any possible catharsis that can so beautifully accompany vulnerability and sharing among others who truly understand.

However, doing such an intensive course that also includes psycho-education sessions, as well as one-on-one sessions with highly trained psychiatrists and psychologists, has helped Martin to better understand the complicated beast that is OCD.

'It's much better than when I was at my worst. Absolutely. Because now I'm able to function. I can eat now and I can take care of myself and I can work enough to pay rent and I can have this conversation with you. So, yeah, my life is so much better.'

He pauses. 'Still, after all these years, I still . . . It still hurts. And I still cry out to nobody in particular, "Why the fuck is this happening to me? Why is this happening to me?"'

Martin says that he's considering doing the intensive program again in the near future. In the meantime, he's using his creative skills to disrupt the false narratives around OCD. He's written a chapter about his experience in *Try Not to Think of a Pink Elephant*, a collection of stories about OCD, and is currently writing a screenplay that uses comedy to explore the often-dark themes that OCD can dredge up.

'OCD has been, and still is, the butt of a joke. So, it's really helpful to do that with positive intentions when your goal is to actually educate or reveal something true, rather than to just point out how weird it is that someone is doing this thing. Fundamentally, humour is an essential part of how I deal with the thought . . . because if you don't laugh, you cry. And I've cried.'

Chapter 3

THE FIRST TRY

I've always found that psychologists' rooms have a peculiar smell. I've never been able to work it out. Is it the aroma of fear? Shame? Perhaps it's the lingering stink of body odour from the sweat that leaks from our pores when we're trying to untangle our lives in front of a stranger. Some psychologists try to mask the stench with scented candles or dusty bottles of diffusers, but it never works. It's as obvious as the discomfort you're trying to conceal when you walk into the room for the first time.

When I was around fifteen, my parents gently encouraged me to seek professional help. My inner turmoil was spilling out, and they were at a loss to know how to help me. However, it would be another four years before I decided to follow their advice. Taking that step would mean having to admit so many things to myself—and to a complete stranger: that I couldn't handle everything on my own; that I was mentally unwell; and that things needed to change. All of these probably sound obvious, but to stay afloat during these turbulent times, I felt like I needed to have a sense of control—admitting these things would mean surrendering, and that was unknown. Suffering felt safer.

The first psychologist I ever saw worked in an office on a leafy street in an inner Melbourne suburb. My initial session was on the afternoon of a humid autumn day in 2006. I was in my first year at university, and I was floundering. My sanity was slipping, and the facade I'd so deftly built was crumbling one panic attack at a time.

I hadn't slept much the night before and had skipped uni classes because I couldn't relax. How honest was I going to be? What would she think of me if I started to discuss my obsessive thoughts about being gay? Surely she'd either think I was a homophobe or suggest that maybe I was gay. Then what would I do? Would she be right? If I told her that I'd spent most of my childhood being worried that I had AIDS, she would just think I was crazy. What if she sends me to a mental facility? As you can probably tell, the uncertainty of what I'd face in a psychologist session seemed almost more unbearable to me than dealing with my (as yet undiagnosed) OCD on my own. So, I decided that, for the first few sessions at least, I'd be very general and vague. I'd shimmy around the edges of my thoughts and test her to see how trustworthy she was, before subjecting her to the murky alcoves of my mind.

I sat in the silent waiting room, aggressively picking at the skin on the sides of my nails, while sneaking looks at the other patients and wondering how long they had resisted therapy for. I thought: *Maybe this is what I need?* I've been managing to keep my head above water for years, but I was getting tired, and I couldn't tread water for much longer.

Soon a well-groomed, grim-faced, middle-aged woman with bouncy, Jennifer Aniston hair called out my name. I walked in, and before I was ushered to an oversized green chair directly facing her normal-sized chair, the smell hit my nostrils. I looked around, trying to find where it was coming from. A dead possum? A dirty nappy in the bin? WHAT WAS IT? But the psychologist just clasped her hands together, waiting for me to sit down. Resisting the urge to open one of her windows and throw myself out into the fresh air, I looked at the box of tissues placed on a stool next to my chair. *Well, I won't be needing any of them*, I smugly thought to myself, except for perhaps covering my nose so I'd only breathe through my mouth. I didn't want to cry in front of a stranger. I knew that if I started then I probably wouldn't stop.

'Before we begin,' she said, 'I need to lay out some ground rules. I'm your psychologist. I'm not your doctor, I'm not your friend, and I'm not your mum.'

She continued to reel off things that she was 'not', but I'd already tuned out. Perhaps I was an overly sensitive teenager, but the line 'I'm not your friend' stung. It wasn't like I'd come to therapy thinking that I'd be BFFs with the person treating me, but I wanted to feel welcome. I wanted to feel secure. Getting to this point, sitting in this room, took so much mental and emotional strength. I didn't want to be here, and yet here I was, because there didn't seem to be an alternative at this stage. But in order to feel safe enough to make a follow-up appointment, I needed empathy and warmth. I needed someone to tell me that I was okay. That I was a good person. That I was trying my best, and it wasn't my fault.

Perhaps she was ticking off her checklist of 'nots' because she thought that was exactly what would create a safe space. But it quickly felt very unsafe to me.

As it turned out, I did need the tissues. When she asked me, 'Why are you here?' in a slightly accusatory tone, a wave of emotion crashed over me—and I promptly burst into tears. I couldn't work out if they were caused by the years of mental torture that I'd endured, or feeling completely unwelcome in this reeking, gloomy room, knowing that this person was not, in fact, my saviour.

OUTTA HERE

I stumbled through the rest of the year, barely present in lectures, dodging my way out of most social events and agonising over any sexual activities between Dan and me. My parents urged me to find another psychologist, but I stubbornly ruled that out after the last experience. *I'll figure it out,* I told myself. *Once I hit my mid-twenties, everything will fall into place.*

Tips for taking the first steps in getting help

Making the decision to receive help for mental illness can be daunting for anyone, but there's often an added complexity when you have OCD. The thoughts that taunt you are often so weird, dark or violent that the last thing you want to do is admit to having these thoughts in case the person you confide in confirms your worst fears and thinks you're crazy, dangerous or perverted. This is understandable. However, the truth is that you don't need to deal with this on your own, and help is available. Here are some tips that will encourage you to take the first step.

Read or listen to the stories of others with OCD

Sometimes, the very first step in healing is knowing that you're not alone in your experience. There are so many great OCD resources out there, and many of them have been created by people who have OCD. For a list of books and podcasts, turn to the Resources section at the end of the book.

Visit a doctor with knowledge about OCD

Seeing a general practitioner (GP) is a sensible first step, as they are the person who provides the Mental Health Treatment Plan that will allow you to receive subsidised treatment. But speaking to a trusted and empathetic GP can also build up your confidence if you feel reluctant to speak to a stranger about your intrusive thoughts and/or compulsions. Without you needing to divulge too much, a good GP can recognise the symptoms of OCD, validate your experience and help you find expert help.

Find a professional with experience treating OCD

If you can, try to find a mental health professional who has experience in treating OCD. Talking to someone about your innermost thoughts and feelings can be daunting, so it's vital that you find someone who will be non-judgemental, patient and knowledgeable. Understanding OCD will be crucial to managing it. It's also important that this person has experience using exposure and response prevention (ERP) therapy. Look up their website or give them a call and ask specific questions about how they treat clients. I'm saying this as someone who *hates* picking up the phone and talking to strangers, so I know it's not easy! But at the end of the day, you want to find the right person to treat you, and you deserve to have someone who knows what they're doing.

Enjoy anonymity

Any good psychologist, psychiatrist or counsellor will take your anonymity and confidentiality very seriously. They are bound by ethical guidelines to protect your privacy. Your OCD will tell you that any professional you speak to will report you or lock you up when they find out what is going through your head. Don't listen to it! Your OCD is a bully, and you've been tormented for too long.

A note about barriers to treatment

It's hard enough to find the right help if you have OCD, but if you add in any kind of marginalisation—cultural, economic, social or geographical—then this makes the process significantly more difficult. I've been in the privileged position of not having to face these barriers, but I know that many people in our society do. Finding a mental health professional with whom you feel safe—not only physically and emotionally safe, but also culturally safe and accepted—is important to the recovery process. For more information on finding mental health professionals, turn to the Resources section at the end of the book.

These thoughts will slow down, and one day they'll stop. I now look back with incredulity at my optimism that this hell would abruptly end. But in that period of my life, this optimism helped me to keep going.

I passed my uni subjects, but barely. It was hard for someone who was used to getting top marks and high praise for everything academic. I knew that I needed a break from my studies. The well-worn path of taking a gap year to go travelling seemed like the only logical option. If I stayed in Melbourne, then I'd drive my poor mum crazy with my persistent 'what-if' scenarios, which were often sexually explicit. We both knew that the reassurances she was giving me were wearing off more and more quickly, just like heroin hits become less effective over time.

A friend of mine, Ella, whom I hadn't seen for years but was still in touch with, was moving to Byron Bay in the new year for a few months before travelling to Europe for the rest of the year, and she asked me to join her. Although I've been racked by anxiety for most of my life, I'm pretty good at making spontaneous decisions that often end up backfiring. So, without weighing up the pros and cons of jetting off on a whim with little money, I booked my ticket to Byron and, from there, an around-the-world ticket that would have me back in Melbourne in eleven months' time. Surely the thoughts wouldn't follow me around the globe?

The thing is, if you don't know what the problem is, you have no ability to face it. You're not living in denial, because there's nothing tangible to deny. I was stranded in this strange no-man's-land of knowing *something* was wrong but having no tools to fix it. It just seemed easier to distract myself with grand plans.

Dan and I both knew that our relationship wouldn't survive a hiatus of that length. We were very much in love, but we were so young, and smart enough to know that our high-school romance was like a delicate bubble: it looked pretty and well-formed, but any outside force would instantly pop it. So, we decided to break up.

On a chilly, dreary Melbourne day in July, Mum held a gathering for friends and family a few days before I was to leave for Byron. Everyone wanted to know what my plans were, and I also wanted to know what my plans were. Deep down I knew that I was running from my exhausting and repetitive reality, but at the time I framed it as 'a good opportunity to travel and meet new people before getting stuck back into uni'. As one of my aunties was leaving, she gave me a hug and then looked at me sternly.

'Just try to enjoy this, okay, Pen? Because it seems to me as if you can never really enjoy anything,' she said, with a hint of condescension in her voice. I was taken aback by this unexpected and forthright comment. I managed to force a pathetic little laugh, but inside I felt deeply hurt. Mainly because I knew she was right. I thought that I'd been fooling everyone for twenty years. Hadn't I projected a laid-back image of someone who loved to have fun? I wanted to be that person. But it's impossible to truly enjoy a moment when your mind is trying to convince you that you're a monster who doesn't deserve to have fun.

SELF-COMPASSION AND OCD

Feeling as though you're a 'bad person' or you're not worthy of experiencing positive emotions is common among those with OCD. When you spend much of your life telling yourself that you're weird or depraved, over time you start to believe it. However, this doesn't make it true. It was only once I was diagnosed with OCD that I started to realise that I'd always put things 'on hold' when I was going through a bad OCD patch. Whether it was planning a holiday, figuring out my next career goal or organising a fun activity, it would have to wait until the OCD settled down again.

When I ask writer and filmmaker Martin Ingle about how OCD has affected his creativity, he thinks about the question for a while before answering.

'Well, I think for a long time it destroyed any creative impulse I had, because it made me feel like I didn't deserve it and that everything was pointless. I had dreams about being a creative person and doing vulnerable stuff that's embarrassing to talk about,' he says with a bashful smile.

'And then when OCD came along, it's like, "Well, if these things about you are true, then you're fucked mate. There's no point in pursuing any kind of dream. You don't deserve anything like that." And for years, that's what it did. It flattened me; it flattened any desire to create something, because I felt I didn't deserve it.'

Kimberley Quinlan, an Australian psychotherapist who specialises in the treatment of OCD and related disorders in California (and hosts the podcast *Your Anxiety Toolkit*), has written a book that aims to give people with OCD the tools they need to harness self-compassion while going through ERP treatment. *The Self-Compassion Workbook for OCD* was born from her own experience of using self-compassion as the cornerstone for overcoming an eating disorder. Quinlan guides readers through daily self-compassion practices and helps people to lean into fear and uncertainty using self-compassion and ERP. For ERP to be effective, she believes it must address how self-criticism and self-punishment reinforce the obsessive-compulsive cycle.

Quinlan mentions equality as a core concept of self-compassion: every single person is equal in their worth, and we are all deserving of self-compassion. This makes me think of all the beautiful people I've met over the last few years who've experienced OCD. For all their resilience, grit, humour and intelligence, I've always noticed an obvious lack of self-worth. They're always quick to see others through a compassionate lens, but they rarely apply this boundless empathy to themselves.

Ben Crowe, a professional mentor and—most notably—mindset coach to tennis champion Ash Barty, talks at length in one of his popular Mojospresso videos on YouTube[1] about the importance of building horizontal relationships. He says that if we put ourselves below or above others (in a vertical relationship) and don't see ourselves as equal, we automatically lose our authenticity. By attaching our self-worth to rankings, or comparing ourselves to others, we're telling ourselves the story that we're not enough.

The problematic narrative that we're often imbued with from a young age is that if we do good things then we *are* good, and if we make mistakes or a bad decision then we *are* bad. This leads to people with OCD believing that if they have bad thoughts, then they're a bad person. But this is just not true. It took me a very long time to realise that we're allowed to have any kind of thought, feeling or urge. We're not our thoughts, and bad or weird thoughts don't make you a bad person. 'This faulty calculation is where shame is born and thrives, perpetuating a false narrative about who you are, your worth as a human being, and what you deserve,' Kimberley Quinlan writes.[2]

Once I learned just how unimportant thoughts are, I felt a sense of freedom—but I also felt somewhat cheated. It was like I was suddenly let in on a joke that everyone else had been laughing at. How could I have not known this? Thoughts had dictated every part of my life for 31 years, and NOW you're telling me they don't matter? It's not uncommon to feel a deep sense of loss during your OCD recovery, because you can't help but think about all the minutes, hours, days, months and years that have been dominated by this monstrous disorder. However, this cycle need not continue. This is where self-compassion can also be helpful. Clinical psychologist Dr David J. Keuler puts it beautifully in his book, *Healing from Obsessive-Compulsive Disorder,* when he talks about forgiveness as a necessary component of compassion. 'Be forgiving of your mind for its betrayal of peace, for its unwanted thoughts, images, emotions, urges and sensations . . . [C]ompassion that expresses itself as caring attention, sympathy, warmth, tenderness and tolerance all kindle the wisdom of the brain to heal from OCD.'[3]

A DIVIDED SELF: BEHAVIOUR AND YOUR BRAIN

Clinical psychologist Dr Andrea Wallace often hears her clients talking about a 'divided self'.

'People with OCD will often talk about the difference between the thinking self and the feeling self. Logically, they know that their obsessions aren't true. But then there's this other big part that makes them feel like they are.'

This relates to psychologist Dr Jonathan Grayson's points, described earlier, about the *feelings* of certainty. So, we now have two experts making it very clear that logic won't change feelings. I wish someone had sat me down and explained this to me when I was a child. Or a teenager. Or even a 25-year-old woman.

If we can't use logic, then what can we use?

'So, what I talk to people about is the idea that the feeling self really pays attention to the way that we *behave*,' continues Dr Wallace. 'No matter what we think, no matter how much we will logically try to make sense of the world, if we are behaving like we are in danger, or like we're a bad person, then we will feel that way.'

Dr Wallace often notices that her clients will use compulsions as a form of self-punishment. They will actively deprive themselves of anything good, because they feel like if they're actually 'dirty' or 'bad' or 'crazy', then they can't possibly experience fun or peace or pleasure as these things are inconsistent with their sense of themselves. Hearing Dr Wallace's explanation is a light-bulb moment for me. My compulsions always felt like a form of self-flagellation, but I'd never connected this to the negative feelings I was having towards myself.

'We need to get people to behave as if they're innocent, behave as if their thoughts don't mean anything and as if they're worthy and lovable so that they can feel that way,' she continues. 'You are teaching yourself in every moment, just by the way that you behave. You're teaching yourself who you are. And you want to teach yourself that you're worthy and you're allowed to just be, and your thoughts are allowed to just be.'

Or as Dr David J. Keuler put it when talking about the 'neuroplasticity' of the brain: 'Change your behaviour and your brain will change in turn.'[4]

THE PITFALLS OF PERFECTION

Perfectionism is a word that comes up a lot in any discussion of OCD. Many people with OCD describe themselves as perfectionists who create unrealistic expectations for themselves. In his book *Freedom from Obsessive-Compulsive Disorder*, Dr Jonathan Grayson discusses how perfectionism can be pursued for its own sake, or in the process of carrying out compulsions to achieve that 'just right' feeling. He uses the example of the specific agony that is felt when someone has carried out their compulsion, but then they need to do it again because the 'just right' feeling doesn't quite feel perfect.[5]

Kimberley Quinlan discusses imperfection as another core concept of self-compassion. She firmly believes that striving for perfection only leads to suffering. Even if we do achieve some form of 'perfection' every now and then—whether it's a perfect score in a test, or that feeling of completion after carrying out a compulsion—the suffering and distress will continue, because we feel like we need to maintain this standard in the future.

To let us off the hook, Quinlan gives us permission to aim no higher than a B– in life. This might make some people feel sick with anxiety, but her rationale is sound. 'Endlessly aiming for an A+ will only set you up to be critical of yourself and continuously dissatisfied and disappointed. Setting realistic expectations is one of the most compassionate things we can do for ourselves. Life gets a whole lot better when you drop the A+ mentality and aim for a B–.'[6]

This attitude doesn't mean that you can't aim high—because you can. But Quinlan encourages us to weigh up the pros and cons of being a perfectionist. If it's causing distress, exhaustion or negative self-talk, is it really worth it?

GOING NORTH

After disembarking from the plane at Ballina airport, having listened to the Missy Higgins song 'Where I Stood' about 40 times, I found myself climbing into the cabin of a ute that my friend, Ella, had organised to pick me up. I didn't know the guy driving it (I later learned that she barely did, either), but I was young and naive enough to only question something if I truly felt like I was in danger. This Byron local seemed friendly enough. Looking back, I cringe at how bemused he must have been by yet another Melburnian arrogantly blowing into his patch of paradise.

Humming along the Pacific Motorway with the winter darkness creeping across the horizon, I started to feel a heavy homesickness in my belly. To fight it off before it settled, I kept telling myself that I was doing the right thing and that this exotic adventure would take me a million miles from my worries. My hands were shaking, and I'm sure the bloke driving the ute was wondering what the hell such an uptight southerner was doing in a place like Byron.

He dropped me outside a basic yet cool-looking youth hostel on the edge of the town, and I felt relieved when I saw Ella rushing out the door to greet me. I gave her a hug, hoping she could sense my anxiety and would tell me that I'd made the right decision. Her eyes struggled to focus on my face, and I could tell immediately that she was stoned. Nothing she was saying made any sense, and I started to wonder if the ute was still in sight so I could ask that guy to take me back to the airport. But before I could check, she rushed me inside and introduced me to her friends, including a New Zealander who was trying to outrun his university debt, and a French chef who looked far too old to be staying at a hostel.

Although I'd been travelling north all day, I had a feeling that everything was about to go south.

I got up early the next day to hike up to the lighthouse, and briefly felt buoyed by the sunshine, the bronzed bodies, and the heady scent of salt air mixed with coffee floating from the main street. I was filled with the positivity that often accompanies the early hours of a beautiful day. But walking past so many gorgeous, willowy bodies, and hearing snatches of carefree, raucous conversations as I passed cafes and shops, I began to feel very out of place. The people of Byron strolled around with a bohemian ease and confidence, which I knew that I could never pull off. To try to quieten my insecurities, I grabbed my iPod and turned up Silverchair's 'Straight Lines', ironically almost bumping into a sun-bleached surfer sauntering down the street.

A few days later, Ella told me that she had arranged a trial for me at the restaurant where she was working. I needed a job and was grateful, but I was paralysed by anxiety and home-sickness, as well as regret for abruptly ending my relationship with Dan. Almost every person that Ella had introduced me to so far was male, about twenty years older than us, with a somewhat creepy demeanour. They all put on a show of being easygoing guys who had forged a new and successful life in this eastern point of paradise, but I kept wondering what they had screwed up or whom they had fucked over to get here. I hoped that a job would help me snap out of my negative mindset and start living in the moment.

After a night of drinking and smoking joints, I woke up late, knowing I had a few hours before my trial started. I made myself a tea and started reading the stack of magazines Ella had bought. Once I'd read everything except the sealed section in the *Cleo* magazine, I hesitated. I usually avoided anything sex-related in books or magazines in case it triggered more intrusive thoughts. But I was too hungover to do anything else, so I kept reading.

One of the first articles in the section was a lesbian confessional, written by a woman who had cheated on her boyfriend. It was one long, graphic retelling of her mind-blowing oral sex with a woman she had met at a club. As I was reading it, my heart rate began to increase, and my breathing became shallow. I kept re-reading it and asking myself the same questions: 'If I'm finding this story arousing, does this mean I'm gay? Is she gay? Did she end up leaving her boyfriend? Will I end up just like her? Am I living a lie? Will I end up alone?' I thought that if I read the article enough times, the answers would burst out of the page, and I'd be able to gather enough evidence to prove to my brain that I was different from this woman. But the more times I read it, the more panicked I became. Suddenly, my hands began to shake, and my breathing became so shallow that I started to feel dizzy. But this panic was infused with anger, and for some reason I walked over to the kitchen sink and smashed the tap with my right fist. Blood poured out from my clenched, white fingers, and I dropped to the floor. I felt like I was going to pass out, so I did what I always did when I was in distress—I called my mum.

The very next day I was on a flight home to Melbourne. Confused and defeated, I stared out of the window and wondered what I'd tell everyone. I'd had a goodbye party with all my friends and family, where everyone wished me well on my 'grand adventure'. My adventure where my thoughts weren't supposed to follow me. Now I was coming home less than a week after arriving in Byron, and I felt like a failure. Like a boxer who had taken a beating, with a (literally) bloody fist and a (metaphorically) bruised ego. But the confusing and infuriating fact was that I was beating up myself. No one else was hurting me. I was in the ring with my own mind, and I was coming off second-best.

Chapter 4

THE INTERLUDE

In a daze of depression and shame, I kept my head low when I arrived back in Melbourne, only contacting a few friends and sheepishly telling Dan that I 'just wasn't ready to take a big trip'. We resumed our relationship, but from that day forward it felt slightly awkward. There was so much that wasn't being said between us, which created a tear in the relationship that would only keep ripping.

Without going into much detail, I told my parents about my panic attack in Byron Bay. My dad suggested that I get a referral to see a psychiatrist. I made an appointment with someone I found online, and my dad came with me for moral support. However, once I stepped into the psychiatrist's office, I felt more alone than I had in a long time. It all felt so clinical, and it started to dawn on me that if I was here, then it meant that there was something very wrong with my mind. I now understand that there hasn't ever been anything *wrong* with my mind, just something different, and I think that's an important distinction to make.

The psychiatrist was an older man, probably in his sixties, with a grey beard, large 1980s-style glasses and a cheerless demeanour. I didn't let myself cry during this appointment, because I knew that there was no way he would be able to console me if I did. I kept it brief, and danced around the details of my worries. I explained that I'd experienced a panic attack and was used to living in a heightened state of anxiety. I told him that I'd often get thoughts that would loop in my mind and wouldn't stop. His immediate, monotone assessment was that I had anxiety and perhaps some OCD-like tendencies. He told me to start on a daily dose of 50 milligrams of sertraline (Zoloft®)—a selective serotonin reuptake inhibitor (SSRI) antidepressant medication—and I'd most likely see a significant decrease in my anxiety and feelings of panic within a couple of months.

The psychiatrist had dropped the phrase 'OCD-like tendencies' so casually and dismissively that I hadn't asked any questions about it. All I knew about OCD at that stage was that it caused Kate Ritchie's character in *Home and Away*, Sally Fletcher, to aggressively wash her hands for a few weeks when she was having relationship troubles in the early 2000s. I didn't wash my hands obsessively, but there was a part of me that wished I did, because that didn't seem as confronting as the thoughts I was having. In my mind, that would be a more 'acceptable' problem to have. No, OCD didn't make sense. Maybe it was just something he value-added to any anxiety diagnosis, like the barista who plonks a marshmallow on top of your kid's babycino with a wink.

I'd like to say that I was completely fine with the idea of taking medication, but this wasn't the case. I felt like a failure. I felt defective. My brother had been taking a combination of meds for the past few years to combat his depression, so how would Mum and Dad feel now that *both* of their kids were on medication? Would they be ashamed? They both assured me that they were anything *but* ashamed, and all they cared about was our happiness.

Happy seemed like a stretch at this point, but I decided to take defeated and defective over panicked and anxious. Now that I know much more about medication and OCD, I barely think twice about taking my tablets—but at the time it felt like I was giving in, or even giving up, to some degree.

My dad strongly encouraged me to see a new psychologist, and because I didn't want to go back to the stern psychiatrist, I conceded. I found a lovely psychologist called Cara, who guided me through some of the side effects I was likely to feel over the next few months, and assured me that medication was the right option. She was a kind, middle-aged woman with a ready smile. Her warmth softened my disdain for psychologists and convinced me to give therapy another try. Luckily for me (I thought), I was armed with an anxiety diagnosis that would give me plenty to talk about, without having to dive deep into my shitstorm of thoughts.

The night I started to take the little white pills, Dan and I went to see *The Lion King* at Her Majesty's Theatre in the city. I'd mentioned to him a few days before that I'd be starting medication for anxiety, but we hadn't discussed it in any detail. As we were sitting in our seats, surrounded by a buzz of excitement and chatter, Dan pulled out his phone and told me that he wanted me to read an article he'd found on antidepressant medication. I was impressed that he'd done some research and was hoping this would calm my nerves. I quickly realised that this wasn't the case. The heading of the article read: 'Why antidepressants stop you from falling in, or feeling, love'. My heart skipped a beat. I looked over at him, confused and searching for an explanation. Then the lights went down, a shadow fell across his face, and the iconic Swahili 'Circle of Life' chant began.

I talked to Cara in detail about starting antidepressant medication. She helped me to sift through the shame I was feeling, and encouraged me to view the process like taking antibiotics for an infection: it wasn't a negative thing, it just *was*. She armed me with printouts flagging all the possible side effects I might experience. Night sweats, decreased libido and insomnia were all medication side effects I was expecting. What I didn't expect was a feeling of 'numbness'. It felt like someone had come at me with a gigantic nail file and aggressively shaved down my edges. It wasn't a bad feeling; it was just foreign to me. I was used to feeling high highs and low lows, but now it felt like I was a submarine gliding through still waters, neither rising to the surface, nor sinking to the bottom.

Fortunately, within about two months the panic had significantly subsided and the undercurrent of anxiety that I was so used to feeling had slowed down. I was able to be more present in my day-to-day life, and although the obsessive fears still haunted me, their grip was less aggressive. I'd lost some of my spark for sure, but when that spark can so easily turn into a fire, I was just relieved to be feeling more 'normal'.

Singer Sara Bareilles explained her experience of starting antidepressants for anxiety on the podcast *We Can Do Hard Things*, saying, 'I always felt like my sadness was my identity. It's part of how I see the world . . . and I felt like if I abandoned that sadness, somehow I was abandoning my essential self. But I actually came back and I was like, "Oh my God, I'm here. Here I am." This person can laugh . . . I just was scared to try. And I'm so grateful that I did because the relief is as wide as the universe.'[1]

I think about this explanation often, because we rarely hear about starting medication as a positive thing—but for so many people it can be life-changing. I'm not suggesting that medication is the only answer. For many, it's just one part of the solution, or perhaps no solution at all. But the more we can peel away the stigmas attached to medication for mental illness, the more freedom people will feel to try it as an option, and to see it as a tool for maintaining wellbeing, rather than as a sign of weakness or dysfunction.

With this new feeling of relative calm, I got a false sense of security and decided to stop seeing Cara. We'd talked a lot about 'calming strategies', and she'd drawn multiple diagrams of the brain to explain the ins and outs of anxiety, but once again, I was too scared to go into detail about my obsessions. I'd dipped my toes in ever so slightly—and she, like the psychiatrist, had thrown around the phrase 'OCD-like tendencies'—but I'd never completely unveiled the extent of my looping thoughts. The fact that my panic had subsided felt like enough, so after one of our sessions I told her I'd email her about the next time I was free to come in, and never got back in touch.

PREFERRED MEDICATIONS

When I ask psychiatrist Dr Scott Blair-West, Medical Director of the OCD Program at The Melbourne Clinic, about whether SSRIs are still the preferred medications to treat OCD, he says that they're often the *first* choice. He mentions that certain studies suggest clomipramine (Anafranil®)—a tricyclic antidepressant—is slightly better, but as it works differently from an SSRI, it can come with more serious side effects.

We know that each of these medications affects a chemical called serotonin, which is used by the brain as a messenger.

OCD and medication

It should be noted that the following information relates to adults, not children. For information about children with OCD and medication, turn to Chapter 12.

Medication can be a complicated choice for some people, and for others it's straightforward. Various factors need to be considered, and when you combine this with the weight of the societal and cultural taboos that have traditionally been attached to taking medication for mental illness, it can be a fraught decision. However, like most facets of mental health, conversations around medication have become more open, and there's an increasing amount of research about what medications work best for various disorders.

According to the website of the International OCD Foundation (IOCDF), around seven out of ten people with OCD will benefit from either medication or exposure and response prevention (ERP). And those who benefit from medication tend to see their symptoms reduce by 40–60 per cent. Many psychiatrists and therapists believe that combining medication and ERP is the most effective approach to treating OCD.[2]

Consulting with a professional

If you're considering taking medication to help treat your OCD, the first step is to see a GP. If they have a strong knowledge of and interest in mental health management, they may be able to prescribe a medication for you. In Australia, doctors don't need any special training in mental health to practise as GPs; however, some may have extra qualifications, and others might have gained valuable experience from working in specific environments or communities. You are absolutely within your rights to ask your GP about their experience and qualifications, and if they feel comfortable managing mental health issues. They may want to refer you to a psychiatrist; if this is the case, then ask your doctor to help you find a psychiatrist with a background in managing OCD.

For more information about how to find a mental-health friendly doctor, you can visit The Black Dog Institute website.

Kinds of medication

SSRIs—selective serotonin reuptake inhibitors—are traditionally used as antidepressants. They are also widely thought to be a good option to treat OCD symptoms.

SSRIs work by increasing the level of serotonin (a chemical that helps to regulate the mood) in the brain. They block the reabsorption of serotonin into neurons, which allows for more serotonin to be available to pass messages between nerve cells.

Alternatives to medication: TMS, ECT and DBS

In some cases where medication and therapy aren't helping with symptoms, a medical professional may suggest alternative treatment options, such as transcranial magnetic stimulation (TMS), electroconvulsive therapy (ECT) or deep brain stimulation (DBS).

TMS is the least invasive option, using magnetic fields to stimulate nerve cells in the brain, whereas ECT and DBS require anaesthesia (and DBS involves surgery). Research results vary when it comes to the effectiveness of each treatment option in reducing OCD symptoms. These options will only be put on the table when first-choice treatments have been unsuccessful.

If your brain doesn't have enough serotonin, then the nerves in your brain might not be communicating well. Adding these medications to your body can help to boost your serotonin and get your brain function back on track.

Generally, when treating someone with OCD, Dr Blair-West starts with prescribing an SSRI medication. If that doesn't work, then he may try another SSRI; if that isn't successful, then he will look at an SNRI (serotonin and norepinephrine reuptake inhibitor).

'The SSRIs really are designed to work primarily and pretty much solely on serotonin neurons in the brain. And they generally do. The other group, SNRIs, actually have a double action: they work on serotonin, but they also work on noradrenaline, which is another transmitter, probably more known to be related to depression than OCD,' he explains.

Individuals respond differently to different medications, which is why it's so important to embark on the medication journey with an experienced medical professional. It can be difficult to predict which ones may work, and some of it will be trial and error. Specific medications may be recommended if you have pre-existing medical issues or if you're taking other medications. It should be noted that not all antidepressant medications will be effective for treating OCD symptoms. Additionally, higher than expected doses of SSRIs are often needed to successfully treat OCD symptoms.

SSRI and SNRI medications don't work immediately. Often it can take a few weeks to a few months to notice any significant changes.

When I ask psychologist Dr Jonathan Grayson about his clients and their attitudes to medication, he says that people often underestimate just how much the medication can help.

'They get better and they go, "Okay, I don't need meds, because I was a mess before that." Then they go off the meds and discover, "Oh shit, the meds were doing something." A lot of people don't like the idea of taking medication. And I say, "I understand that, but your body doesn't really care what you want."'

It can be confronting to realise that you may have to rely on tablets every day for the rest of your life, and it certainly took me many years to accept this. It won't be the case for everybody, but if it is your reality, it's okay to feel upset about it and it's also okay to change your view on medication over time. We live in a society that tends to hold strong, rigid views about taking medication for mental illness, but try to drown out the sound of the crowd and think about what might be best for you.

Antidepressants for OCD

The IOCDF lists eight medications that work well for OCD:[3]

- citalopram (Cipramil®)*
- clomipramine (Anafranil®)
- escitalopram (Lexapro®)
- fluoxetine (Prozac®)
- fluvoxamine (Luvox®)
- paroxetine (Aropax®)
- sertraline (Zoloft®)
- venlafaxine (Efexor XR®).

* Note: The Australian TGA warns against using high doses of this medication.[4]

Side effects

All medications have the potential for side effects, and everyone reacts differently, so it's important to discuss these with a medical professional. Medications prescribed for OCD aren't addictive, and are *generally* well tolerated by most people. However, some common issues caused by the SSRIs that are recommended for OCD include (but aren't limited to):

- insomnia
- restlessness
- nausea
- feeling agitated or shaky
- low sex drive
- dry mouth.

Clomipramine (Anafranil®) can also have more serious side effects, which are worth discussing with a medical professional.

It's common for many of the side effects to lessen or disappear after the first couple of months. And the severity of the side effects can depend on the dosage. It's often recommended to start on a low dose and gradually increase it, to limit the side effects.

Time frame

The advice on the IOCDF website is to give a particular medication about three months before you decide to change. It's crucial that the medication is taken daily, and it can be very dangerous to stop taking medication suddenly. If you want to stop taking medication, it must be done gradually, and preferably with the guidance of a medical professional. Stopping medication suddenly can cause withdrawal symptoms, such as headaches, nausea and electric shock-like 'brain zaps', as well as the return of symptoms (relapse). Tapering off over a longer period can reduce these symptoms.

While some people may be able to stop taking medication for good after six to twelve months, others may need to be on medication for years—or even forever.

Harriet's story

When Harriet's daughter, Elena, was six years old, she was so fearful of throwing up that she started refusing to go to school in case she caught gastro. It got to the point where she couldn't even say the word 'vomit'. Harriet made an appointment with a psychologist, who diagnosed her daughter with emetophobia (the fear of vomiting) and generalised anxiety disorder (GAD).

When the Covid-19 pandemic hit, Elena spent most of the next two years learning remotely, and Harriet noticed that her symptoms settled. At age nine, when Elena was back at school and had her first excursion since the end of lockdowns, she became overwhelmed while getting onto the bus and had a panic attack.

Soon after, Harriet started noticing little rituals Elena was doing before getting into bed every night. She would have to make sure that her slippers and socks were in the correct position in her room and her school uniform was laid out correctly. Harriet talked to her daughter about these routines, and eventually Elena told her mum she believed that if she didn't perform the rituals, certain family members would die.

Elena was subsequently diagnosed with OCD. However, within the space of a few weeks, things started to spiral.

'It was really shocking. Things unravelled so quickly. Every few days a new compulsion was added to her bedtime routine. She would have to repeat the process multiple times until it was "just right"; if someone interrupted the routine, she would have to start again,' explains Harriet.

At night, Elena would have to ensure that items on her bookshelf and bedside table were in the correct position and blinds were positioned a certain way, she would have to touch particular items in her room in the correct order, and she and her mum would have to say goodnight in a certain way. On top of the bedtime routine, Harriet noticed that Elena was starting to hold her breath in the shower and refused to drink water at school for fear of it being contaminated.

If Elena didn't perform the compulsions, she would become visibly distressed. These rules were controlling her every move, and they were starting to take their toll on the whole family. Elena was often irritable and angry, and at the time Harriet couldn't understand her daughter's difficult emotions.

There's often no logical connection between the ritual and the feared outcome in this kind of OCD, called Magical Thinking OCD. It can be incredibly frustrating for those close to the sufferer, because it can seem so bizarre and absurd. Elena was also experiencing 'just right' obsessions, which are thoughts or feelings that something isn't quite right, or that things feel incomplete.

'Now that I understand OCD so much better, I realise that she was in such serious distress because she really believed that if she didn't perform her compulsions, either she or someone she loved would die. That's heavy for a nine-year-old, so of course she was upset!' exclaims Harriet.

Seeking help

She noticed that Elena's compulsions were starting to become more obvious to the outside world. Every time Elena would eat something, she would then need to tap her mouth a certain number of times to get that 'just right' feeling, as well as to ensure that nothing bad would happen to anyone she loved.

Harriet was desperate to find the right treatment and support for her daughter. The psychologist suggested that Elena should go on medication, but they couldn't get in anywhere to see a paediatrician or psychiatrist to obtain a prescription.

Unsure of what else to do, Harriet called the Child and Youth Mental Health Service (CYMHS) at the Austin Hospital. After a few weeks they got an appointment, and it was decided that they should wait a few more weeks until taking the medication route.

Elena's psychologist looked particularly worried when she pulled Harriet aside after a session with Elena. She told her that Elena had asked her how her family could possibly love her with everything she was putting them through.

'My heart broke into a million pieces hearing that,' recalls Harriet. 'No one wants their child to feel that heavy, and it was clear that her self-esteem was starting to really be affected by the OCD.'

The decision was made to start Elena on a very low dose of fluvoxamine (Luvox®). It wasn't made lightly, but Harriet felt like there weren't any other options. To Harriet's relief, things improved dramatically within a week.

'Elena was doing about a page and a half's worth of compulsions. But once she started the medication, it dropped to just a handful. I felt like I had my daughter back. It was unbelievable,' says Harriet.

Although Harriet was initially concerned about starting her daughter on medication, for fear that she would experience negative side-effects, thankfully Elena hasn't experienced any adverse reactions so far, and after five months of taking it she continues to do well on a low dose.

Harriet doesn't feel comfortable talking to many people about starting Elena on fluvoxamine, due to the negative perceptions that some continue to hold about medicating kids.

'You hear some people saying, "Oh why medicate your kids?" But I've been through it and I know what crisis she was in, and you just do what you can. In the end I felt that not medicating her was probably worse because she was in a really bad place. She was really overwhelmed and scared and stressed,' Harriet says.

Finding her tribe

Since Elena's psychologist didn't have much experience with ERP, Harriet felt like it was solely up to her to ensure that Elena was doing exposures at home. It wasn't until she came across the courses at Natasha Daniels' AT Parenting Survival Online School that Harriet felt like she finally had access to more tools to support Elena's therapy. As someone who had spent countless hours searching the internet to better understand OCD but felt like she was hitting dead ends, the resource was a revelation for Harriet.

'Navigating all the information available online was incredibly overwhelming. But I've found the Natasha Daniels resources hugely helpful. Elena even joins monthly meetings online with other kids from around the world who have OCD. She understands it so much more now, and can separate herself from the disorder,' she says.

Harriet has joined the AT Parenting Community, which she says has provided her with support, understanding and information, in a world where mental health is still so stigmatised.

'I can't just talk about this with anybody. People don't get it. Being part of the parent community means that I can talk to others who have been through similar experiences and ask them questions when I feel a bit lost,' explains Harriet.

Harriet and Elena try to create an exposure hierarchy together every month that sits on the fridge. When Elena completes an exposure, she accrues points, and once she reaches her goal for the month, she can get an award (this month it's a small voucher for an online game). Although it's never easy, Harriet is always there for her daughter, cheering her on and encouraging her to stay on top of her OCD.

Recently, Elena celebrated her tenth birthday. Although her OCD hasn't disappeared, it's well managed.

'It's been so rewarding to see her spark come back over the last few months and her personality shine through again—it's a real joy,' says Harriet.

Chapter 5

THE SILENCE

Over the next few years, it felt like everything—and nothing—changed. I lived for a while at the University of Melbourne's Ormond College, resumed my studies, finished my degree, travelled around South America with some girlfriends and came home to a job working in the communications department of the university. During much of this time, particularly while I was residing in the college, I barely had any alone time during which my obsessive thoughts could throw down an anchor. I was functioning relatively well until I got back to Melbourne and started working in a job where I sat at a desk for most of the day.

Dan and I had broken up again while I was at uni, and we had been apart for three years. For reasons I still can't fully articulate, we eventually got back together.

EAT PRAY OBSESS

I felt like Elizabeth Gilbert in *Eat Pray Love*, but before she did all the eating, praying and loving. It was more like the agonised version of Elizabeth at the start of the book, when she's having a meltdown and finds herself on her bathroom floor talking to a god that she doesn't believe in. I wasn't talking to a god, but I did find myself on the tiled floor in the tiny upstairs bathroom of Dan's house, wondering what the hell to do next. I'd been on medication for five years but was once again tortured by obsessive thoughts, and no amount of positive thinking, exercise or yoga was making them budge.

I was 25, in a relationship that made me more sad than happy, and coasting along in a job that I'd show up for in person, but never in spirit. The themes of my obsessive thoughts varied between health fears (do I have cancer?), relationship questions (am I into this enough?) and hit-and-run fears (did I just run over somebody and not notice?). My journals were filled with lists, lame quotes and naive, positive self-talk all willing myself to be more disciplined. Just get up earlier each day and exercise! Don't attach any meaning to your thoughts! Learn a new skill! JUST BE BETTER FOR FUCK'S SAKE, PENNY! GOOD VIBES ONLY!

But, lying awkwardly on the floor between the shower and the toilet, I felt hope slipping and my toxic positivity dissipating. *Something is very, very wrong*, I thought. Dan was sleeping soundly metres from the sliding door to the bathroom, but I couldn't go to him. Our relationship was already on a knife's edge, and I'd never opened up to him about my internal struggles. My parents were trying to help my brother overcome his struggle with depression; as willing as they would have been to help me, I didn't want to add to their distress. In hindsight, what I needed to do was to find a psychologist with whom I felt comfortable enough to divulge my embarrassing and repetitive thoughts, but it all seemed too hard. I'd tried that already—twice in fact—and felt like I hadn't made much progress. So, I did the next logical thing: I booked myself in for a ten-day silent-meditation retreat in country Victoria. If I couldn't snap myself out of this hell through positive thoughts and to-do lists, then I'd meditate my way out of it! Elizabeth Gilbert would have been proud.

After a two-week holiday in Japan over the Christmas break with Dan, I arrived back in Melbourne and felt emptier than I had before we left. My excitement level from being in a place I'd wanted to visit for years was tempered by the fact that I was travelling with someone whom I knew was no longer in love with me. Our interactions were as frosty as the Japanese guesthouse windows I'd stare out of, wondering why we were still pretending. Both of us realised that a break-up in a foreign country would be too disorientating. And both of us knew it would end back on the familiarity of home soil. Which it surely did.

In the days between tearily moving back to the family home and heading off to Woori Yallock for my ten-day retreat, I got stoned with my friend, Frankie, and was flashed by a man at St Kilda Botanical Gardens. Things were unravelling at speed. *At least I'd soon be enveloped in silence*, I thought. In desperation, my flawed logic was telling me that I could hit pause on my pain and panic for ten whole days.

Luckily, I'd learned enough about Vipassana retreats from my dad—who had been doing them since the 1980s—to know what to expect once I got there: waking up to the eerie and unwelcome sound of a gong at 4 a.m.; ten hours a day sitting on your bum; no food after 1 p.m.; no talking or eye contact; and lights out at 9 p.m. Vipassana has no ties to religion or particular groups—it's all about using the sensations of the body, starting with the breath, to increase awareness, peace and balance. I knew that this wasn't going to be a walk in the park, but I felt like I needed to take dramatic action to effect significant change in my life. The official Vipassana website notes that this ancient, nonsectarian technique 'aims for the total eradication of mental impurities and the resultant highest happiness of full liberation'.[1] FULL LIBERATION? YES PLEASE!

It was all good in theory, but fighting OCD demons while doing a Vipassana meditation retreat is like a heroin addict doing . . . well, a meditation retreat. You are left with nothing but your thoughts, and there's nowhere to turn if you start to spiral. No phone, no writing materials, no TV, no books. Just meditating, eating and sleeping. Not only was I dealing with the sorrow of losing someone from my life whom I'd dearly loved for the last eight years, but—without any distractions—I was also now besieged by my fears at all times of the day and night. Rather than sitting with the discomfort that my thoughts would provoke, for the first few days I got stuck in mental loops, trying desperately—as I always did—to think my way out of uncertainty. I obsessively counted down the hours until the tenth day, when our phones and car keys would be returned. I wasn't sleeping, because I had no way of suppressing my thoughts with my usual distractions (mainly wine). I was stuck in a daze of boredom and despair.

However, having no access to anyone from whom I could get reassurance, and no internet to try to disprove the insane theories in my mind, it was—without me even knowing it at the time—a hardcore, and ultimately unsuccessful, version of ERP therapy. So many memories resurfaced, from years of thinking and fearing and worrying and panicking. But the speed of the thoughts outpaced my ability to 'work them out', so I had no choice but to endure the prickling pain they caused. On the last day, I was disappointed that I hadn't yet reached full liberation. But I was also buoyed by the relief of surviving the gruelling course, and dizzy with excitement about doing something as mundane as ordering a soy latte from a cafe.

MINDFULNESS

We've all heard the term 'mindfulness' ping-ponged around. It's become something of an empty buzzword, and the very utterance of it may have you rolling your eyes. I get it. Thanks to Instagram influencers, whenever I hear the word I still can't help but recoil. However, the reality is that mindfulness can be extremely helpful—I'd argue essential—in overcoming OCD. This certainly doesn't mean that you need to rush off to book a ten-day meditation retreat, but it's worth exploring in any way that appeals to you.

According to Jon Hershfield and Shala Nicely, mindfulness is 'non-judgemental awareness of the present moment'.[2] In their book, *Everyday Mindfulness for OCD*, they guide the person with OCD through a step-by-step journey towards not only managing OCD, but also living *joyfully* with OCD—through mindfulness and self-compassion. They explain that mindfulness is about observing the world in the present moment, without evaluating it, running from it or wishing it were different. It is the ability to create distance between ourselves and our thoughts, without pushing them away. But the authors make an important point: mindfulness is a way to *experience* the world, not something you *do* to it. I find this distinction helpful, because it makes mindfulness something bigger and more useful. It's something that can be incorporated into your everyday life.

It's important to know that mindfulness comes from ancient Buddhist principles, and it has been practised and passed down for millennia. Mindfulness, meditation—whatever you want to call it—was never intended to be something that only *certain* people can use. At its core, it's a nonsectarian practice that can be adopted by anyone. To delve deeper into the Eastern origins of mindfulness, turn to the Resources section at the end of the book.

96

Mindfulness from an Indigenous Australian perspective

Mindfulness isn't something that belongs to one culture or religion. It's worth remembering that different cultures practise mindfulness in various ways. When it comes to Aboriginal and Torres Strait Islander cultures, there's an intrinsic connection between good mental health and concern for the Earth. Gunaikurnai man Jamie Marloo Thomas found that every wellness program he encountered omitted any reference to the Earth. So, he co-founded Wayapa Wuurrk, a practice based on ancient Earth mindfulness.

'To have a healthy mind, body and spirit, you have to have a healthy Earth. If we just tread more lightly on Mother Earth, she will look after herself. Otherwise, we're not going to destroy the planet, we're going to destroy ourselves,' he explains.

Mindfulness and OCD

So why am I banging on about mindfulness? The short answer is that people with OCD aren't great at staying in the present moment. In their book, Jon Hershfield and Shala Nicely talk about how those with OCD are 'noticers'. We can see things in minute detail, which can be both a blessing and a curse. 'This enhanced attention to detail in the mind lends itself to creativity, humour and ingenuity. Being able to enjoy the fruits of a noticer's mind necessitates being able to shoulder the burdens of that same mind,' they explain.[3] When we're worrying about an obsession or performing a compulsion, we're either stuck in the past or projecting ourselves into the future. We are *rarely* in the moment.

Until I read *Everyday Mindfulness for OCD*, I never understood how mindfulness and ERP therapy were so intertwined. I won't go into too much detail here (you'll learn all about ERP in Chapter 8: The treatment), but in a nutshell, ERP involves purposefully triggering a fear; feeling any thoughts, emotions or sensations that arise; and then mindfully *not* performing a compulsion to try to neutralise the anxiety. According to Hershfield and Nicely, ERP requires mindfulness skills to resist the powerful urges of which we've been a prisoner for so long.[4]

Clinical psychologist Dr David J. Keuler describes OCD as a 'disorder of resistance'. We learn to react to our triggers with a powerful biological impulse: the fight, flight or freeze response. He suggests that mindfulness can help the person with OCD to find relief. 'Mindfulness interventions slow individuals down, teach them to pause, to sit with their aversion, and to select responses that heal rather than hinder. In states of mindlessness, individuals with OCD rarely find relief.'

Dr Keuler has a fascinating backstory. A clinician who has treated OCD for over two decades, several years ago he found himself fighting his own OCD demons. He knew how to treat others, but facing his own OCD was another battle altogether. He went through a steep learning curve, studiously observing his OCD and combining his more mainstream clinical approach with ancient principles focused on the transcendence of pain and suffering. He became mesmerised by the depth of this ancient approach, and taken by the possibility of being free of suffering. 'Individuals were seated in front of me each day asking for guidance to reduce their suffering. Eastern philosophy had something very important to say, and I felt an obligation to listen carefully,' he explains.

While ERP and mindfulness complement each other very well, Dr Keuler recommends that people begin their treatment journey focused on approaches with solid empirical evidence behind them, such as ERP, and then adding mindfulness-based interventions if necessary. This isn't to say that there's no evidence for the effectiveness of mindfulness; in fact, research has been extremely promising when it comes to mindfulness and treating illnesses such as OCD, depression and anxiety. However, compared to research on more clinical approaches such as ERP, it's less substantial. But this is an area that is gaining momentum in the research world.

MEDITATION AS A TOOL

Meditation is one technique you can use to help you to stay in the present moment, without judgement or expectation. Some people are put off by the idea of meditation; however, I've found it to be a helpful tool. There are many different kinds of meditation, and it's worth doing some research to work out what technique appeals to you. *Everyday Mindfulness for OCD* has a number of useful exercises to gently introduce you to meditation and pull you back from the throes of compulsions.

Clinical psychologist Dr Andrea Wallace often uses mindfulness techniques with her clients to help them to adopt the 'role of witness to their thoughts, emotions and sensations' rather than identifying with them.

'When I'm working with clients, I ask them to notice that their thoughts are just mind stuff, just things that arise in the mind. The brain is a creative instrument, which comes up with all kinds of creative things that can scare us. We can watch that, and in the watching we are being mindful.

'The same approach is used with respect to unwanted sensations—especially the groin response [attention and anxiety that might lead to heightened sensations in your groin area]. We notice it instead of identifying with it. Instead of interpreting it as "me", we identify it as something we witness our body doing. This function is as innocent as the function of our kidneys and pancreas. A bodily sensation cannot be immoral, just as creation of insulin isn't immoral,' explains Dr Wallace.

Be mindful of expectations

I've been exposed to meditation since I was a little girl, because my dad has been practising Vipassana meditation since the 1980s. However, it's only recently that I noticed my approach to it would always be from an evaluative standpoint: 'That was a terrible meditation; I was thinking the whole time' or 'I need to get *better* at meditating.' I was totally missing the point, and being a classic OCD perfectionist. Bringing your distracted mind back to the present moment *is* being mindful. You can't 'win' at meditation. As Jon Hershfield and Shala Nicely explain, '"Good" meditations are just meditations you feel good about. They don't have specific qualities that are better than meditations you feel bad about.'[5]

Difference between mindfulness and thought suppression

It's probably not surprising that trying to suppress a thought will often lead to increasing the frequency of that thought. If I were to tell you not to think of a purple kangaroo, chances are that's the first thing that would pop into your head. Therefore, it's critical not to link mindfulness or meditation with thought suppression. The goal is never to *stop* a thought, it's to notice it and try to detach any meaning from it. And if you ever come across a therapist who advises thought suppression as treatment for OCD, run in the other direction.

STILL BODY, ACTIVE MIND?

Many people with OCD, including myself, have turned to practices such as yoga or meditation to help with their heightened feelings of anxiety. I started attending yoga classes when I was eighteen, yet I often found that by the end of a class I was more tangled up in my obsessions than I was before I sat on the mat. It wasn't until I tried a more active form of yoga—Bikram—that I was able to immerse myself in the class (to an extent) and feel like I was able to (slightly) relax.

When I ask Dr Andrea Wallace about this, she explains that OCD usually takes up whatever space is available to it. This is why people with OCD often find that holidays or weekends are the hardest times.

'People with OCD tend to be concerned that their free time will be "ruined" by unwanted intrusive thoughts. Therefore, when we have free time, we check for the thoughts to ensure they aren't present. In order to check for thoughts, we must create them, and so we find the thoughts are present. This can be heartbreaking.

'Some people find it helpful to engage in more active forms of relaxation, giving the mind something to occupy it. For some people, this might involve physical activity (for example, hiking, dancing, kayaking), and for others it might involve creative play (for example, making art or music, playing games, taking a class) or socialising,' she says.

This isn't to suggest that activities such as yoga or meditation aren't useful—they certainly can be. But it can be helpful to start with more active forms of these endeavours, such as walking meditations or Ashtanga yoga, especially if you find that your mind is easily triggered when your body is still for long periods.

Dr Wallace says that we need to start expecting our unwanted thoughts, images, urges and sensations to bubble up when we're not busy. Assume that they'll come with us to the yoga class, the meditation cushion or the banana lounge in Queensland. She says that we should try to see this as 'predictable and ordinary' rather than a personal failure.

ANCHORS AWAY

I wouldn't necessarily recommend signing up for a meditation course if you're going through a crippling mental illness without any professional help, but luckily for me, it didn't do any harm in the end. However, once I returned home, not long after sculling my third latte, I fell in a heap. The uneasiness caused by my break-up had caught up with me and put a dampener on my new Zen outlook. My life was undergoing so many changes, and I felt exposed, raw and flimsy. I emailed my friend and confidant, Blaise, who was living and working in Nairobi, and his response to my distress has stayed with me ever since.

Me:
Well, things have certainly changed a shitload since I was last in touch. Dan and I broke up a few weeks ago, I've moved back home (which is a new home, because Mum and Dad have moved), I've quit full-time work, and I'm going back to uni full-time. I feel as if almost every anchor in my life has been cut, and I have NO IDEA WHERE I AM!

Blaise:
It's interesting that you wrote that you have no idea where you are, and of course I completely understand where that sentiment comes from. 'Anchor' is such a good word to describe what a partner, secure job etc represents. But the metaphor is interesting, because an anchor is also something that stops you from moving. I don't want to get too Freudian here, but while we rely on those anchors to make us feel safe in the present, sometimes they can make us feel restricted for movement in the future.

I now try to see change—and even discomfort—as a catalyst for growth, where beforehand I saw it as an overwhelming defeat. This is, ironically, one of the lessons of Vipassana (not responding with fear or negativity when something unwanted happens), so maybe Blaise's email came at the perfect time to help me to distil ten days of discomfort. Things were changing, but they had to change. Not only were my thoughts looping because of my (still undiagnosed) OCD, but my actions were looping, too. I kept coming back to things, and people, that were safe and known. Extending myself by doing something that was completely out of my comfort zone made me realise that discomfort is not only inevitable, but also completely necessary.

Chapter 6

UPS AND DOWNS

Trigger warning: this chapter contains references to suicide

I don't know if it was the regular meditation I was doing at least once a day, or the fact that I was now out of a relationship that at times had made me feel unsettled, but about two months after completing the Vipassana course, I went to bed with obsessions (as usual) and woke up without them. Actually, that's slightly misleading: thoughts still entered my head, but they seemed to ping-pong straight out again. I lifted my head from the pillow and felt lighter than I had in a long time. I remained still, waiting for the familiar panic to set in, but . . . nothing.

Feeling deeply suspicious of this sudden sense of peace that had settled into my nervous system, I waited all day for it to morph into a feeling I was more accustomed to: unease, angst or anxiety. But it didn't change. That night when I went to bed—and for the first time ever—I was able to choose what I wanted to think about. I mean, I know that we always have a choice, but up until this moment I'd always felt like I was held hostage by my thoughts, particularly during moments when there were no other distractions. That night I had the most peaceful sleep I've ever had and, once again, I woke up in the morning unperturbed by my thoughts.

What the hell is going on? I wondered, thinking that maybe someone was spiking my daily cup of coffee with a tranquilliser. I tiptoed through the next few weeks, worried that any sudden movements might trigger an avalanche of worries that would once again bury me. But nothing happened. The regular 'what if?' thoughts were still around, but they were more of a whisper than a shout, and I slowly began to disregard them altogether.

Whenever I went on a date and ended up sleeping with the guy, I'd leave the unsatisfying sexual encounter (not to mention dull conversations) unfazed. *That was pretty average sex*, I'd think. And then I'd move on like a 'normal' person. No incessant looping thoughts about why I might not be attracted to men, or a scene-by-scene re-run of the occasion, picking apart every moment that might offer me a clue as to why I didn't love the experience. Just a shoulder shrug. It felt too easy.

Is this how most people experience life? I wondered. Because, if so, it felt like a fucking walk in the park.

PEAKS AND TROUGHS OF OCD

It's thought that there are two 'kinds' of OCD when it comes to the course of the illness: chronic and episodic. Someone with chronic OCD will generally always experience some level of symptoms, even if the severity fluctuates. Episodic OCD only presents for a certain amount of time and is then followed by a period when symptoms disappear, with or without treatment.[1] Most presentations of OCD are chronic, and many people with chronic OCD experience symptoms that wax and wane over time for various reasons.

A study carried out in 2021 investigated why the severity of OCD symptoms seems to ebb and flow throughout the day.[2] It looked at a person's chronotype (whether they're a morning person or a night owl) and how their symptoms presented over a seven-day period. It found that during times of higher alertness, the person experienced a reduction in their symptoms. So, those who function best in the mornings tended to experience worsening symptoms at night when their alertness levels were compromised. This sounds straightforward and logical, but it can help to be mindful of when OCD symptoms are likely to flare up or settle down.

Another recent study looked at symptom fluctuation in anxiety disorders (including OCD) during the menstrual cycle.[3] Interestingly, it suggests that for people with OCD and post-traumatic stress disorder (PTSD), the perimenstrual period—from roughly the week prior to the week following menstruation—can be a time of heightened vulnerability to anxiety symptoms. This is thought to be due to fluctuating hormone levels throughout this time.

Clinical psychologist Dr Andrea Wallace suggests that OCD tends to peak when things such as stress and sleep deprivation are in play. She also notes that certain OCD themes can coincide with significant life events, causing OCD symptoms to flare up.

'People tend to have particular themes that are problematic, such as having an overdeveloped sense of responsibility. So, events that are associated with those themes—for example, living through a pandemic or having a baby—can cause OCD to peak,' she explains.

At the end of the day, however, Dr Wallace highlights the fact that wherever compulsions are performed, OCD will be found. And while it can be helpful to be aware of the things that might exacerbate your symptoms, the OCD flame will continue to burn as long as compulsions are fuelling it.

'For instance, if a new parent begins to perform compulsions in response to their unwanted intrusive thoughts, OCD symptoms will increase. If they drop the compulsions, the symptoms will drop away,' she says.

A NEW LOVE

Hugh and I first reconnected a few weeks after I returned from living and working in Geneva for six months. I'd briefly dated Hugh's brother, Josh, in high school and had bumped into Hugh a few times over the years. After chatting on

Facebook Messenger over the previous few months, Hugh and I decided to meet up at a cafe in Melbourne's inner north. The catch-up was organised under the pretence of a work opportunity, which was real, but I think that we both knew—or at least hoped—there was real chemistry between us.

Hugh arrived about fifteen minutes after me, and I noticed that he had the same slightly lopsided, swaggering gait as his brother. He had a beaming smile and plonked himself on the chair next to me. Not only did I feel immediately at ease, but I also knew that I wanted to spend more time with this man. I felt an instant connection and attraction to him. We talked about the job he thought I should apply for, with my background in health communication, but before long we were chatting about everything from cricket to meditation. The conversation flowed so effortlessly, and we both quickly realised that we found the same things funny. I wasn't forcing laughs at his jokes; he genuinely had me in stitches. I knew then that I needed to be with someone who made my diaphragm ache from laughing. Both of us left the cafe unsure of what the future held, but certain of the fact that we would see each other again.

Fast-forward about two weeks, and Hugh and I were spending almost every day together. I'd been invited to apply for a permanent job at the organisation I was working for in Geneva, but the thought of being away from Hugh seemed unfathomable. He invited me to join his family holiday in a rented house in

Fairhaven, on Victoria's Great Ocean Road, where I met his parents. We all awkwardly made jokes about the fact that I used to date Hugh's brother when I was fourteen years old. I was particularly keen to impress Hugh's mum, Liz. Her three kids were her world, and she was the moon orbiting around them, never interfering but unfailingly present in their lives. It didn't take long for her, along with the rest of Hugh's family, to quickly accept me into their universe.

Over the next few months, I felt so giddy with love and fulfilment that I started to wonder why I was still taking the little white pills every morning. I hadn't been racked with obsessions for almost a year and, while I often felt anxious, those feelings seemed to pale in comparison to the torture of obsessions, so I felt like it was all manageable. I hated the idea of being on medication for my whole life, and I'd convinced myself that if I went off the sertraline (Zoloft®), I'd regain the career ambitions that had dissipated after the first month of being medicated. For the last year I had cut down to half the dosage I was originally on, and things hadn't fallen apart. I wasn't seeing a psychologist or a psychiatrist, but I was in love! And love conquers all!

Or so I thought. I went from taking 25 milligrams of sertraline (Zoloft®) every day, which is a very low dose, to taking nothing at all. After a few months, I realised how much those tablets were doing for me.

The first few months were manageable. I'd get regular 'brain zaps' or sudden feelings of vertigo throughout the day, but I was expecting those. After all, I'd googled 'What to expect after going off antidepressants?' plenty of times. What I conveniently ignored was the clear warning that suddenly stopping antidepressants can be life-threatening. But considering that many adults with OCD take up to 200 milligrams of sertraline (Zoloft®) per day, I didn't think that 25 milligrams was enough to really affect me if I wasn't on it. I'd been taking the pills for almost eight years at that point, though, and my brain had become accustomed to a higher level of serotonin.

I started noticing little things creeping back into my routines that were annoying but didn't really bother me at first. When I was driving, I'd wonder what it would be like if I shut my eyes for a second. I'd try it. Then I'd wonder what would happen if I shut them for two seconds. I didn't want to do it, but I couldn't stop wondering what would happen, so I thought it would just be easier if I did it. But then I'd have to do it again and again, for slightly longer periods each time. It sounds idiotic, and dangerous. I didn't have any kind of death wish, and it's a difficult compulsion to explain, but I couldn't stop. I'd also regularly clench my jaw, even though—or perhaps because—it was very uncomfortable and hurt my teeth. But again, my brain wouldn't let me stop.

Hugh noticed my anxiety returning when I woke up at his place one morning feeling particularly irritable and slightly panicked. We'd planned to go out for breakfast at a nearby cafe in Fitzroy with two of his best friends, whom I'd never met, and I said that I'd drive. Almost as soon as I got out of the garage, I mounted a traffic island in the middle of the road, which I swear I'd never seen before. Hugh looked terrified to be in the car with me, but he decided not to say anything. When we got to the cafe and were being shown to our table, I knocked over a glass jar filled with sugar that I hadn't noticed in my peripheral vision. It was a chaotic entrance, and the sort of thing I'd usually laugh off. But I felt flustered and annoyed at my clumsiness, and I quickly excused myself from the catch-up, explaining to Hugh's friends that I had a migraine.

ANXIETY AND THE BRAIN'S RESPONSE

What I didn't realise was that, in my high state of anxiety, my brain couldn't differentiate between stress and danger, so it began shutting off the parts that I didn't need for 'survival', such as the frontal lobe. Energy could then be redirected to my limbic system (emotional brain) and my brain stem (survival brain). That's why I was crashing into things, knocking things off tables and just generally feeling like my faculties were out of control. If I'd had more insight back then, I'd have spent some time during these episodes calming my limbic system through conscious breathing, exercise or simply validating my feelings. ('Of course you're feeling this way. It's okay to feel anxious and worried.')

Dr Andrea Wallace regularly comes across clients who view anxiety as dangerous. She says that if we try see our anxiety as more of a superpower, then it will revolutionise the way we experience it.

'What an amazing ability—to have our body produce adrenaline to make our heart race, our breath quicken, to send our blood to our major muscle groups. All of this is the reason we've survived as a species. It's perfectly safe to be flooded with anxiety. It's not something that actually puts us in danger.

'I encourage people to try to make friends with the feeling and sit alongside it. Try to notice all the aspects of the feeling and then welcome it and give it some space just to hang out, knowing that when you stop resisting it, your level of suffering will decrease,' she explains.

THE DRUGS (DO) WORK

As irritating and tiring as the anxiety was, it didn't tempt me to go back on the medication. I kept telling myself that I felt more like 'me' again, whatever that meant. I'd broken free of the medication shackles, and I was proud of myself. I hadn't taken the pills for about three months when Hugh and I stayed at Palm Cove in Far North Queensland during the Easter break. On our first evening, as we were sipping cocktails at a bar overlooking the turquoise waters of the Coral Sea, I felt elated. Holidays were usually the time when my obsessive thoughts would escalate, and yet, at that moment, I felt calm and in control. *I've beaten it*, I thought.

But OCD has a devilish tendency to slap you down when you least expect it.

What's the difference between anxiety and OCD?

There are lots of different kinds of anxiety disorders, from panic disorder (PD) to post-traumatic stress disorder (PTSD); however, below I'll be talking about generalised anxiety disorder (GAD).

While there are crossovers between GAD and OCD (many people with OCD experience huge amounts of anxiety, and it's common for those with GAD to experience recurrent thoughts), there are significant differences between the two illnesses.[4] Some three million Australians are living with an anxiety disorder, which makes it the most common mental illness in Australia (a whopping one in four Australians will experience anxiety at some point in their life).[5]

Symptoms of GAD[6]

The anxiety or worry is associated with three or more of the following symptoms (only one item is required in children):

- feeling restless or on edge
- being easily fatigued
- having difficulty concentrating
- frequently feeling irritable
- suffering from disturbed sleep
- complaining of muscle tension.

Differences between GAD and OCD[7]

- Those experiencing GAD will usually worry about real-life concerns (school, friendship, career, financial issues), whereas those who have OCD will generally be consumed by thoughts that are irrational or unlikely. (*Am I sick? A paedophile? A murderer?*)

- Those with GAD will generally worry and ruminate about their distressing thoughts, whereas those with OCD tend to worry and ruminate, as well as perform certain compulsive behaviours (that may or may not be overt) to neutralise their anguish.

The very next day I was kicking back on the hotel couch, flicking through TV channels, when I settled on a movie from the early 2000s. There was some kind of sex scene in the back of a car. I'd watched plenty of sex scenes on TV over the previous year, and none of them had cause me to spiral, but for some reason I started to become fixated on a familiar stream of thoughts. *Do I enjoy sex enough? If I don't, does it mean I'm not into Hugh? But I want to be with Hugh. Will I have to leave him?*

These thoughts kept swirling around and around my head, and I was no longer enjoying the tropical weather, or the aroma from the nearby seafood restaurant wafting through the open window behind me. I was being abruptly pulled back into the OCD maze, which had no way out—just one dead end after another. I tried to calm my mind with a wine, but it only made things worse. I told Hugh that I was tired and went to bed early, so I could lie down and keep thinking my way through my 'problem'.

The next morning, Hugh got ready for an early run before breakfast. I knew that exercise often helped to interrupt my obsessive thought cycle, so I decided to go with him. He could tell that I was being less talkative and more distracted than usual, but I kept explaining that I was tired. Hugh soon got the message that I didn't want to talk, and we ran in silence along the sand.

It's back, I realised. *It's fucking back.*

My heartbeat quickened, and my breathing became shallow. Before I knew it, I was clutching at my throat and yelling to Hugh that I couldn't breathe. It wasn't because of the running, as I'd hardly broken a sweat. I was having a panic attack, and my body felt like it was shutting down. Hugh tried gently to sit me down and encouraged me to breathe. The problem was that I was breathing too quickly and hyperventilating. After a few minutes of listening to Hugh's reassuring voice, the panic lessened and I was able to breathe normally again. We were both shaken by the experience, and I admitted to Hugh that I was starting to experience repetitive thoughts and feelings of anxiety again. He suggested that perhaps I should think about going back on medication, but to me that felt like failing. If I went back on medication now, wouldn't I just have to try to get off it again a few more years down the track? I'd come so far, so I'd push through.

My mental state deteriorated in sync with Melbourne's weather as autumn turned to winter. It happened in three stages: anxiety, obsessive thoughts and then depression. I felt more irritable at work and within my relationship than usual. I started doubting all of the decisions I was making, and my self-esteem vanished altogether. Within weeks, the negative self-talk was drowning out any of the positive things that were happening in my life. I asked myself why Hugh wanted to be with me, and why I was such an impostor in my role at work. I convinced myself that no one liked or respected me, and that I was a fraud. It felt as if there was a dense, black cloud over my head, and I started to actively push people away so they didn't have to experience the shadow that the cloud was casting over me.

One day after work, while I was waiting for a tram on Collins Street, I spoke to Hugh on the phone and basically told him to leave me alone because I wasn't worth the effort. Then I slumped onto the footpath. I'd seen depression drain my brother's spirit. I knew what it looked like, and I suddenly realised that it was happening to me. I wearily dragged my heels from the tram stop to my parents' house, where I was living. I hoped that they would be there, and that they would ask me what was wrong, so I wouldn't have to volunteer the fact that I was falling into a deep well of sadness.

They had just returned from a hike in New Zealand and were happy I was home so they could show me a slide show of their holiday. After each photo, my dad looked at me, his face beaming. He didn't register my hostile attitude or take any notice of my pathetic grunts of approval. He just kept going, as dads tend to do when in slide-show mode.

'I think I'm deeply, deeply depressed!' I blurted out, while Dad was explaining to me that he was always the one lagging at the back of the pack, even though *he* thought he was one of the fittest people there.

I could see all the muscles in my mum's body tense up, and Dad and I both knew that he would have to be the one to tackle my sudden confession. As an intensely empathetic person, Mum is very good at mirroring other people's emotions. But what I needed at this moment was a calm, steady voice telling me what to do. He sat down with me and used gentle questions to try to break down the anger and defensiveness I was holding on to. After a while, he suggested that I go back on the sertraline (Zoloft®). I agreed immediately and decided to start on my original 50-milligram dosage again the very next morning. Within a day, the vice-like grip of depression had loosened. The negative thoughts quietened right down, and I could get through a dinner with Hugh without thinking of ways I might sabotage the relationship.

I felt raw and exhausted from the last few months. Popping the tablets out of their packet again each morning, I felt a mixture of defeat and relief.

TREATING OCD AND DEPRESSION

The International OCD Foundation (IOCDF) suggests that 25–50 per cent of people with OCD will also have a major depressive episode, which involves feeling low for at least a few weeks as well as experiencing symptoms such as feelings of worthlessness or hopelessness, appetite issues, sleep problems and low energy.[8] In many cases, depression follows OCD largely because of how troubling and exhausting OCD can be. Sometimes OCD and depression can begin at the same time; however, it's unlikely for depression to precede OCD (in other words, OCD can lead to depression, but there's no research suggesting that the opposite is true).

Because OCD can cause depression, in many cases the depressive symptoms will ease once the OCD symptoms are treated. When I ask psychiatrist Dr Scott Blair-West about the connection between OCD and depression, he says it's something he sees all the time in the OCD inpatient clinic he runs in Melbourne.

'We have a new program every three weeks in our hospital program. Around four of the seven people currently admitted were actually quite depressed when they came in. The question we always have to answer is whether the depression is going to be resolved if we treat their OCD effectively. And that's usually the case. We're usually better off treating the OCD first,' he says.

In his research, Jonathan Abramowitz, Professor and Associate Chair of Psychology at the University of North Carolina at Chapel Hill, has found that one of the best predictors of treatment outcome for OCD using exposure and response prevention (ERP) therapy is the patient's level of depression.[9] He discovered that seriously depressed people won't do as well as non-depressed or less depressed people. This makes a lot of sense. ERP can be hard, tiring work, and if you're already experiencing feelings of hopelessness and sadness, you'll be far less motivated to start and continue with this kind of therapy. Professor Abramowitz's research found that the most effective way to start treating depression and OCD is to use elements of cognitive behavioural therapy (CBT) to challenge the person's negative thoughts. Once the person is feeling motivated and strong enough, ERP can be introduced to combat the OCD symptoms.

If someone is feeling so depressed that they can't engage with or gain benefits from CBT or ERP, they may need to start antidepressant medication (or look at altering their current medication). In some cases, they'll need to attend an inpatient facility or hospital for intensive treatment.

In their book, *Everyday Mindfulness for OCD*, Jon Hershfield and Shala Nicely discuss the benefits of using self-compassion to help manage depression and OCD.[10] They point to research suggesting that self-criticism often predicts depression, relapse of depression and a poorer outcome from treatment. Therefore, they highlight the importance of normalising the experience of depression if you have OCD, and giving yourself permission to feel the way you do. A simple way to practise this is to validate your own feelings to yourself. But don't do it lightly—talk to yourself like you would a best friend and *really* empathise with yourself: *I'm so deeply sad and depressed, but it's SO understandable that I'm feeling this way. Living with OCD is extremely hard. It can be absolute torture. It's common for people with OCD to also experience depression. And I'm allowed to feel this way.*

OCD AND SUICIDE

'Giving up is so incredibly tempting.'[11]

This is a quote from Brianna Smale, one of the people interviewed about OCD during an episode of ABC TV's *You Can't Ask That* in 2021. Most interviewees discussed the fact that at some point in their OCD journey, they had thought about suicide.

Because depression is commonly associated with OCD, there's a significant risk of suicide among people with OCD. A study carried out in Sweden over four decades found that the risk of dying by suicide was ten times higher for those with OCD than for the general population.[12] I'm not saying this to scare anyone, but it's important to understand just how serious OCD can be.

THIRD TIME LUCKY

When I started back on medication, I had to make an appointment at the GP to renew my Mental Health Treatment Plan, because I knew that I'd have to start seeing a psychologist again. I didn't have a regular GP or a psychologist, so I was starting from scratch.

Hugh pointed me in the direction of a wonderful psychologist, Jodie, whom he knew professionally. After a few months on the waiting list, I had my first appointment. In the waiting room, I noticed a gigantic collection of tea bags next to a kettle.

Suicidal OCD

It's important to distinguish between suicidal ideation, which is thinking about or planning suicide, and Suicidal OCD, which is intrusive thoughts about suicide and repetitive behaviours used to calm the anxiety that these thoughts provoke. Suicidal OCD is closely tied to Harm OCD. People who experience Suicidal OCD *don't* want to harm themselves, and these thoughts cause them significant distress.

People who experience Suicidal OCD can find it difficult to seek help, as they often worry that the person they confide in will think that they're a serious risk to themselves, confirming their worst fears. Finding a GP or therapist with experience in OCD can make reaching out for help much easier.

Having always equated any kind of hot drink with comfort, I welcomed this thoughtful addition.

After a few minutes, a petite woman with light brown hair, kind eyes and a big smile opened her door and called me into her office. She asked me to choose a seat, but I was too busy staring at all of the green objects in the room. Green chairs, green table, green lamp and green candles. I couldn't work out the reason behind all this green, but I was impressed with her commitment to the theme.

Just like the first psychologist I saw years earlier, Jodie asked me why I was here. Tears immediately started to stream out of my eyes, and snot dripped from my nose. However, her reaction was different. She looked at me with compassion, patiently waiting for all of the fluids to stop flowing from my face, offering me tissues and telling me to take my time. I could tell that she was a mother, because she had such a protective maternal force emanating from her.

Before the session, I decided that I'd only talk about anxiety, medication and the depressive feelings I'd experienced. They were all 'safe' topics. If I decided to make any follow-up appointments, I'd start talking about the obsessive thoughts.

Jodie agreed that it was a wise decision to be back on the sertraline (Zoloft®), but she said that she could support me down the track if I wanted to try going off medication again. It wasn't until years later that I started to feel more at peace with the fact that medication was vital to my wellbeing, and I began to shed the feeling of defeat that I'd always associated with taking antidepressants.

I saw Jodie every few weeks for about eighteen months. In that time, I felt listened to, cared for and understood. However, I kept skirting around the real issues that I needed to talk about. I was still experiencing all kinds of obsessive thoughts, which would lead to constant compulsions. Now that I was happily in a relationship, I started to experience more intrusive thoughts about whether I loved Hugh enough (later, I'd learn that this is Relationship OCD).

With Jodie, I learned a lot about anxiety and what happens to the brain when we feel anxious. She was always busily drawing diagrams on her whiteboard, and I'd enthusiastically nod along and take photos of the diagrams with my phone—but I'd never look at them again. Subconsciously, I kept thinking that if I ignored the obsessive parts of my mental illness for long enough, then they would fade away. If I didn't translate them into reality with my voice, then they would surely cease to exist.

It wasn't until I had my first child that I finally gained the courage to face my OCD head-on.

Chapter 7

THE CIRCUIT BREAKER

I've never said this to anyone before, but I think that one of the reasons I decided to start trying to get pregnant was because I was unhappy in my job and thought that a baby would give me time to hit the pause button and think about what I really wanted to do with my career. Anyone who's had a baby will laugh hysterically at the assumption that a baby can give *anyone* time to do *anything* (apart from look after said baby).

I'd always wanted kids, and I was sure that Hugh would be an incredible dad. So, we decided to stop using contraception. Both of us expected that it would take six months to a year for me to fall pregnant—but it happened one month later. We were both shell-shocked but also ecstatic.

I'd been regularly seeing a wonderful GP to whom Jodie had referred me, who specialised in antidepressant medication. She assured me that continuing with my current dose of sertraline (Zoloft®) while pregnant would be unlikely to put the baby at risk and would mean I had a better chance of maintaining stable mental health while going through the hormone changes that accompany pregnancy. I'm so grateful to that doctor for giving me that reassurance, and I shudder to think how I'd have managed the prenatal and postnatal periods if I'd tried to go off the medication again.

While the first trimester was a tumultuous ride of highs and lows, I felt much calmer once I hit the second trimester and even noticed that my obsessive thoughts had simmered down. I'm very aware that this isn't everyone's experience, as pregnancy can be a very triggering time for many people with obsessive-compulsive disorder (OCD). But for some reason, I felt lighter (metaphorically; physically, I was enormous) and quite at peace during this period. I'm grateful for this brief ceasefire in my mind, because once Benji arrived, the peace shattered and the battle recommenced.

VULNERABLE TO THE WORLD'S VIBRATIONS

Two days after giving birth to Benji, I was feeling sore and emotional. Hugh was having a nap on the couch with Benji, and my dad could tell that I needed to get some fresh air and caffeine. I'd stubbornly refused any pain medication while in labour and was trying not to think about the agony I'd experienced to birth the tiny person whom we all now loved more than life itself. I was struggling to deal with any tragic news stories I heard on the radio or saw on TV that involved babies or children, and I was besieged by vivid thoughts about something bad happening to Benji.

Dad explained to me—while we were sitting at a little cafe in Hawthorn, on steel chairs that were particularly unsuitable for anyone who had recently had their vagina ripped in half—that once you have a child, you tend to feel more vulnerable to the world's vibrations. These words have stuck with me, because he perfectly summed up how I was feeling. Every little tremor now felt like an earthquake, and I was constantly on alert, trying to protect the tiny heart we had created.

Over the next few months, with a baby who would only sleep after we bounced him on a gym ball for half an hour, Hugh and I started to morph into the zombies from *The Walking Dead*. I felt increasingly anxious, and the obsessive thoughts had come back with full force. I started writing my ridiculous lists again, trying to find my way out of it all with meditation and positive thinking. Three weeks after having Benji, I wrote this entry in my journal:

> My anxiety has really spiked in the last couple of days and
> to get out of my head a bit I thought I would try writing.
> My obsessive thoughts are spinning around and around,
> making me feel exhausted, hopeless and frustrated. I am

trying to meditate each day and use the technique of labelling thoughts and watching them. I believe this is how I will conquer these thoughts and this repetitive cycle. I need willpower and determination.

On reflection, I've never been in short supply of willpower or determination. What I desperately needed was the right professional help.

PERINATAL OCD

'Perinatal' refers to the period from when you become pregnant to a year after giving birth. This can be a time of great upheaval, both emotionally and physically, for those going through it. If you add in a mental illness, it can be extremely destabilising. Perinatal obsessive-compulsive disorder (pOCD) refers to the condition of people who experience OCD symptoms for the first time—or a recurrence of OCD symptoms after a period of remission—during pregnancy or after giving birth. If you have OCD before becoming pregnant you are more likely to get pOCD but it can be triggered for the first time during the perinatal period.[1] It's believed that this is largely due to fluctuating hormone levels, lack of sleep, and big life changes that trigger some people's OCD themes[2] (for example, someone with contamination fears might start worrying about passing on germs to their baby). Symptoms may also change for people with OCD during this period.

The perinatal period is a particularly risky time for people to develop OCD symptoms, with the likelihood being especially high in the first six months postpartum.[3]

The thoughts experienced with pOCD will often revolve around keeping the baby safe and can present as intrusive thoughts about injury, death or sexual harm. *What will happen if I drop my baby? What if my baby drowns in the bath? What if I want to drown my baby? What if my baby stops breathing, and I'm not in the room to do anything?*

It must be made clear that people who experience these thoughts *don't* want to harm the baby. These thoughts are horrific to them, and they often feel ashamed, embarrassed and highly distressed about them.

Compulsions related to pOCD might include constant checking (for example, that the baby is breathing), excessive cleaning and washing to avoid any kind of contamination, seeking constant reassurance from others about the health of the baby, over-attachment to the baby and avoidance of the baby.

TREATMENTS FOR pOCD

It's now recognised that pOCD can seriously affect the health of the birth parent and, as a result, the development of the baby, which is why it is so important to start treatment as soon as possible. Treating pOCD is no different from treating other kinds of OCD, with medication and exposure and response prevention (ERP) being the preferred options. In some cases,

Who gets perinatal OCD?

If you have a history of OCD, anxiety or depression, you're more likely to experience pOCD. Family history of mental illness and any history of abuse are also risk factors. Unfortunately, pOCD is still under-recognised because of the lack of research, and the failure to screen for it at perinatal check-ups. People are also often embarrassed or ashamed about their thoughts, and worry that if they ask for help, their baby will be taken away from them.

It's important to note that fathers or non-birthing parents can also experience pOCD (often called paternal OCD).

sufferers will find it particularly difficult to do ERP therapy, due to the distressing nature of their thoughts and the likelihood that they are sleep-deprived. However, if ERP is done with the guidance and support of an experienced therapist, it can be very effective, and medication can help to maximise the benefits of therapy.

I'll discuss both treatment options below (and ERP in more detail in the next chapter).

Medication

Research into medication and pregnancy is lacking, because of the ethical conundrum of including pregnant people in trials. However, selective serotonin reuptake inhibitors (SSRIs) have the most research behind them for pregnancy and breastfeeding, and they currently appear to be the safest form of medication during the perinatal period.

When I ask psychiatrist Dr Scott Blair-West about taking medication during the perinatal period, he says that the general consensus has shifted dramatically.

'Ten to fifteen years ago it was generally recommended that women stopped [OCD medication] during pregnancy. Now, if you talk to pretty much everyone (obstetricians, perinatal psychiatrists, and so on), the consensus is that you balance the risks against the benefits. And it sounds now as though there's more risk to the baby from the mother being sick during pregnancy than there is from the pills,' he says.

Professor Anne Buist—who has 30 years of experience in perinatal psychiatry—explains that it's not an easy decision for individuals or couples to make, but it's an important one.

'The question I help women and their partners with is "what are the risks to my baby with my illness at its worst, unmedicated, versus being medicated, but well?"'

Professor Buist explains that in weighing up this question, she asks the pregnant person what their illness looked like at its very worst, and whether they feel that they could survive a pregnancy while being that unwell.

It's recommended that you discuss the pros and cons of staying on medication with a GP, psychiatrist or obstetrician, as all medications come with possible side effects. SSRIs taken in the third trimester have been linked to poor neonatal adaptation syndrome (PNAS),[4] where the new baby can have symptoms such as irritability, jaundice, jitteriness and fluctuating temperatures. However, these effects usually resolve within a few weeks.

When I first talked to my GP about taking medication while pregnant in 2016, she explained that sertraline (Zoloft®) was thought to be the safest SSRI—meaning that it had the most research behind it. I ask Professor Buist if this is still the case.

'Yes, just from purely the numbers,' she says. 'With medications like thalidomide [a drug widely used in the 1950s and 1960s], that's very clear. Thalidomide causes limb defects in babies. There's no question. But there's nothing like that with any of the antidepressants. And sertraline [Zoloft®] comes out the cleanest from the research,' she explains.

However, she adds that you need to discuss the dosage you are currently taking or plan on taking when pregnant and breastfeeding, as any medication is likely to be more problematic at higher doses.

Exposure and response prevention (ERP)

ERP is the most effective treatment for pOCD (see Chapter 8). However, the therapy may have to be undertaken alongside medication.

If you're experiencing pOCD but don't have a therapist, try to find an expert in OCD to confide in. Disclosing the intrusive thoughts to someone who understands the illness will ensure that you feel comfortable during the process. For more information on finding someone with OCD expertise, turn to the Resources section at the end of the book.

Tips for the perinatal period

- This isn't always possible, but if you can, consult with a medical professional *before* getting pregnant. Then you'll have a plan of action, and you won't feel like you have to make any hasty decisions. And if you decide to go off your medication or decrease the dosage, it means you can do so gradually and safely.

- Psychiatrists can be difficult to access, and cost can be a barrier for many, so remember that you can start by having a discussion with your GP.

- Continue to consult with your doctor throughout the pregnancy. Professor Buist highlights the fact that medication taken while pregnant becomes slightly diluted by the third trimester, because of the increased fluid in the body. Therefore, some people may need to increase their dose at this stage to get the same effect from their medication.

- If you're already seeing a psychologist, and if your circumstances allow, then continue to see them throughout your pregnancy, and make regular appointments after the baby is born. Most therapists provide telehealth options, which is useful as it can be difficult to leave the house with an infant, especially in the first few weeks. You will find more information about telehealth options in Chapter 10.

- If you don't currently see a therapist, and you're pregnant or plan to become pregnant, do some research to see if you can find someone to support you through this time, or attempt to get on some waiting lists. Even if your OCD symptoms aren't serious, they can spike after the baby is born.

- Continue doing all the things that keep you well when you're not pregnant—such as meditation/mindfulness, exercise (consult a doctor to ensure that you're doing this safely), socialising or listening to music.
- Harness as much support during the perinatal period as possible.
- Work out what your boundaries are once you have your child (for example, the number of visitors you're comfortable having in the first few months). For more information about accessing support during the perinatal period, turn to the Resources section at the end of the book.

FINDING THE RIGHT HELP

One afternoon, I was sitting in one of Jodie's bright green chairs in her bright green office, and I knew that it was finally time to start talking about my thoughts. I was sleep deprived, irritable and feeling increasingly desperate. I began to delve into the history of my obsessions, going into more detail about them than I'd ever done with anyone except for my parents. I braced myself for what Jodie would say, once my confessional was over. Would she think I was crazy? Would she dismiss it as 'just anxiety'? Would she report me to child services for being an unfit mother?

Jodie smiled at me, thanked me for being so honest and then confirmed what I already knew. 'It sounds like obsessive-compulsive disorder. Unfortunately, I don't have much experience in that area, so while I would be happy to keep seeing you, I don't think I would be particularly helpful.' When I asked her if she could recommend someone else, she didn't have any names. 'Perhaps try the website www.findapsychologist.com.'

I felt relieved and panicked all at once. I wondered how I'd ever find help if this well-established and experienced psychologist could only point me in the direction of a generic website. I walked out, feeling grateful for finding someone who had gently and compassionately guided me through the past year, but disheartened that my courage in finally revealing the extent of my obsessive thoughts had only resulted in another dead end.

A few years earlier, I'd come across an article in a magazine written by someone who experienced purely obsessional OCD (aka 'Pure O'). It was shockingly honest, and the author had signed off as 'anonymous'. But it didn't matter to me. As I read about how 'anonymous' had been tormented by intrusive thoughts for years (until they'd found a therapist who did ERP), I finally felt the relief of things clicking into place.

I wasn't the only one.

There is a name for this.

There is a way through.

It would be years before I'd be officially diagnosed, but this was a pivotal moment for me. So, when Jodie mentioned OCD, I wasn't at all surprised. I was relieved.

A week later, I dropped Benji off at his grandparents' house so I could do the grocery shopping. Benji was now nine months old and still waking up between two and six times a night. Hugh was travelling interstate almost every other week. Sitting in the car at the Coles car park that frosty June morning, I felt depleted. I knew that I only had an hour to do all of the mind-numbing errands that come with being a parent, but I couldn't get out of the car. Over the past few months, I'd been noticing myself becoming less present with Benji as the obsessive thoughts crowded my mind, making the moments of parental joy scarcer. I was missing things—the little moments of connection, the smiles, the brief but joyful interludes that make parenting worthwhile, even when most of the time you want to bang your head against a wall. I began to see a future where I was locked in the bathroom, missing all of the big moments of family life. Where Benji would be wondering where I was, banging on the door, asking me why I wouldn't come out. I felt the familiar rise of panic, accompanied by a quickening heart rate and short, shallow breaths. Tears rolled down my face, and the car started fogging up as I struggled to breathe. I grabbed my phone and called my dad.

'Dad, I need help. Like proper help,' I managed to squeak out between hyperventilating breaths. My dad encouraged me to slow down and remember that this would pass, recognising that I was having a panic attack. He patiently waited for my breathing to slow, while gently telling me that I was okay. I told him that I didn't want to be an absent parent, and that my OCD was getting out of control again. Ever the strategic, big-picture thinker, he said, 'Right Pen, what you need is a plan.'

The plan was to do whatever it took to find specialist help in OCD. No more faffing about with a psychologist who may or may not be able to help—I needed someone with proven experience in dealing with OCD. It would be a twelve-month plan, as I searched high and low for the right help, whether that was a psychologist or an intensive inpatient program.

Searching through the website that Jodie had suggested, I couldn't find anyone who had much experience with treating OCD. I googled 'OCD specialists' and found a few dedicated centres around Australia that ran OCD programs, but I couldn't find much else. I needed to widen my net, so I asked family members and a couple of friends if they had any leads on psychologists who treated people with OCD. Within a couple of months, I'd put together a list of psychologists to contact. A friend of my brother was a psychologist, and he knew about a clinician called Dr Andrea Wallace who had proven experience in dealing with OCD. A few days after I contacted Dr Wallace's clinic, the receptionist called and told me that Dr Wallace had a four- to six-month waiting list. She asked if I wanted to try someone else at the same clinic. I was tempted, as I wasn't keen on treading water for six months. But I also knew that I wouldn't be able to handle another failed attempt at finding the right person. So, I decided to wait.

What to do while you're waiting for help

- If you haven't yet, try to find a GP whom you feel comfortable with. Tell them you need a Mental Health Treatment Plan (you'll often need to book an extra-long appointment for this), and ask them for a referral to a therapist who has experience with OCD (and ERP).
- Start to educate yourself by reading books, listening to podcasts and visiting websites dedicated to OCD. For more information, turn to the Resources section at the end of the book.
- If you're employed, ask your workplace if they offer an Employment Assistance Program (EAP). This is a voluntary program that offers employees free and confidential assessments, counselling and referrals. The issues don't have to be work-related, and this could be a good option while you wait to find specialised help.
- If you have private health insurance, give them a call and ask them what extra resources they have regarding mental health support. They may be able to point you in the direction of specialists in your area.
- If you're feeling unsafe, you can contact your local mental health crisis team by phoning your closest public hospital. The team comprises mental health professionals (including psychiatrists, psychiatric nurses and social workers), and is available 24/7. The team members can help you manage the crisis you're in, and then refer you to appropriate services for long-term management. If your mental health crisis is life-threatening, ring 000.

The relief of finding someone who might actually be able to help me took a huge weight off my shoulders. While the following six months were tough, just knowing that there was some hope in the near future felt cathartic. In that time, I started to read about ERP, which kept popping up on websites about OCD treatment. The more I read, the more uneasy I felt. I'd need to face my fears head-on. What would that mean? Could I survive that?

Beck's story

Beck had always been an anxious kid, and she remembers recoiling from intrusive thoughts about her parents dying. But it wasn't until after she experienced a post-joint panic attack following a friend's party in her mid-twenties that her world began to crumble.

Feeling fragile and hung over the day after the party, Beck was chatting with a friend when she suddenly imagined their neck splitting open and their head falling backwards.

What the fuck? she thought. *What the hell was that?*

She had never experienced anything so gruesome and vivid. It shook her to her very core. When the thoughts kept happening, she began to assume she was having some kind of psychotic episode, and was terrified of these unwelcome and alarming thoughts.

'I couldn't sleep, I couldn't eat, because I was like, "Why am I having these thoughts?" I didn't know what was wrong. I didn't tell anyone,' Beck explains.

If you see Beck at a cafe, or chat to her at a party, it's hard to imagine the hell that she has endured. A social worker in her early forties and a mother of one, Beck is always immaculately dressed and one of those people who carries a lighthearted energy into any room she enters. It's not until you ask about her history of mental illness that the years of distress and confusion start to come into focus. Her effervescence is quickly replaced with a pained sincerity.

Unsure of what to do about her thoughts, she booked in to see a psychologist. She was convinced she was schizophrenic, unaware that what she was experiencing were intrusive thoughts, not hallucinations. However, she didn't feel comfortable describing her thoughts to the psychologist, so she was diagnosed with generalised anxiety disorder (GAD), and later bipolar disorder. Unsurprisingly, things didn't improve following these misdiagnoses.

'Then I became afraid. I wouldn't use knives. I was too scared to be in kitchens. If anyone was using a knife, I had to leave the room. But I just kept it all inside and didn't tell anyone what was going on. I just started drinking. And then for the next seven years I just drank and took drugs all the time to cope,' explains Beck.

After years of heavy drinking, Beck joined Alcoholics Anonymous (AA) and got sober. However, a few months into her sobriety, the thoughts returned. But they had taken an even darker turn. When her partner's niece was staying over at their house, and she was changing her nappy, she began experiencing sexual intrusive thoughts.

'It was horrendous. I rang Lifeline. I remember trying to talk to them, but I was just so scared they were going to put me in gaol or something. I lost a lot of weight. I was very, very skinny,' Beck recalls.

A powerful moment

Thankfully, not long after the thoughts began to torment her again, Beck met a co-worker who had been diagnosed with OCD, and who was very open about her obsessive thoughts. She told Beck that she'd had all sorts of thoughts—from obsessing that she would reach into her partner's chest and pull out his organs, to molesting kids. But she was far enough along in therapy to know that *they were just thoughts*—not an indictment of her character. And certainly not anything she wanted to think about, let alone act upon.

'I think, for me, it was probably one of the most powerful moments of my life, and it gave me so much hope. I thought, *Oh my God, I'm not a freak*, because I honestly believed I was. Anytime anyone would give me a compliment, I would think, *Yeah, but if you knew the thoughts that I had in my head, you wouldn't want to be friends with me,*' she explains.

With the encouragement of her co-worker, Beck saw a psychiatrist. She was taken off the antipsychotics that her GP had given her when she was misdiagnosed as having bipolar disorder, and she started on escitalopram (Lexapro®), an antidepressant that's often used to treat OCD. She began seeing a psychologist who had experience with OCD, but he never encouraged her to do ERP. They talked about it, but they never took the plunge and got started.

When Beck found out she was pregnant, she stopped seeing the psychologist. She didn't feel like things had improved much, but she was hopeful that the intrusive thoughts wouldn't reappear.

After a very stressful and high-risk pregnancy, her daughter, Georgia, was born. To her relief, she was perfectly healthy. However, to Beck's dismay, she didn't feel all the heart-bursting joy we're told we should feel when we meet our newborn.

'I was scared of her when she was born. Even the first time I looked at her, I was scared of her. And then I remember driving home from the hospital and my husband was like, "Sit in the back with her." And I remember just looking at her, thinking, *I don't want to sit next to her.* I was really scared of the responsibility.

'I was really fearful and—especially in those first couple of weeks—it was quite awful. I was scared I would break her. But then I started having intrusive thoughts, like really yucky ones. Like the worst ones I've ever had, ever, to this day,' Beck recalls, cupping her face in her hands.

If Beck made a tea or coffee, she would have to put Georgia on the other side of the room, believing that if she was close she would throw the boiling water on her. Fearing she would hurt her baby with a knife, she stopped making dinner altogether. Then one night, Beck was watching the news and she saw a story about a mother who had thrown her toddler in a river and killed her. This was the final straw for Beck, who lived close to a river and would often take her baby in the pram near the water to get some fresh air during the day.

Beck called a postnatal hotline, trying to explain her thoughts to the person on the line, but unfortunately they didn't recognise these thoughts as a symptom of OCD. However, they contacted Beck's psychiatrist and encouraged her to go to a Mother and Baby Unit. This wouldn't necessarily have been a bad thing, as Beck clearly needed help; however, when she got there, the head psychiatrist said that she didn't believe Beck had OCD. She swiftly took Beck off the escitalopram (Lexapro®) and gave her benzodiazepines to help her sleep.

'The treatment was horrendous, and I'm going to lodge a complaint at some point when I've got the strength to do it. I was in there for two weeks, and I was suicidal by the end of it. I'd been ripped off my medication, and I had no access to a psychologist in there,' she explains.

Beck eventually discharged herself. But as she had been relying on the benzos to get to sleep, when she returned home she didn't sleep for four nights straight. Exhausted, unmedicated and with a partner who was working all day, Beck was floundering. She was worse than before she entered the unit, and she felt like she was running out of options. Her baby, only four months old by this stage, needed her mother, but Beck was so petrified of hurting her that she could barely parent her.

Rock bottom

When a thought about putting a drill through her baby distressed her to the point of absolute panic, she called her nearest mental health crisis team. She was taken straight to a different Mother and Baby Unit.

Luckily, this time the psychiatrists listened to Beck and decided to try her on fluoxetine (Prozac®), another kind of antidepressant often used to treat OCD symptoms. After a month, Beck's symptoms had improved; however, once she returned home, she still needed medication to get to sleep. It wasn't until she came across a group-therapy option run by Swinburne University (STOP Therapy) that things started to really improve.

'It was on a Monday night, I remember. And that's when everything got better. Everything. We learned how to do exposure therapies. And the best thing was that we started doing them straight away,' Beck recalls.

At the time, many of Beck's thoughts revolved around knives, so one of the exposures she was encouraged to do during STOP Therapy was holding a knife to the psychologist's neck.

'The psychologist got a big, sharp butcher's knife and told me to hold it against her throat in front of two other people. I was shaking and crying, and everyone was like, "You're doing so well, Beck. You've got this!" Eventually, I started laughing and said, "I'm not going to hurt you." I had faced one of my biggest fears, and it's so weird because it then went away,' Beck says.

Since that time, Beck has been doing individual and group therapy regularly and is still taking fluoxetine (Prozac®). She has good days and bad days, but generally her OCD is well managed. She has a great career, and Georgia is now an energetic, vivacious seven-year-old with whom she shares a beautiful, unbreakable bond, despite the shaky start.

Beck desperately wishes that she'd had access to a psychologist or some kind of peer support when she was in the two Mother and Baby units. It pains her to think that other parents, who are in the most vulnerable period of their lives, might have to navigate the same unpredictable terrain that she had to.

'I wish someone could have told me, "Your thoughts do not represent who you are. They are in no way an indication of what you want to do. You've got this. I was as bad as you, but I've come through. You're not the worst,"' she says.

Chapter 8

THE TREATMENT

My first session with Dr Andrea Wallace was the day after my 31st birthday. I sat in a light-filled room in another old terrace-style office in North Carlton, not far from where I had my first experience with a psychologist twelve years earlier. Sitting in the waiting room, I could smell that familiar nauseating scent of sweat and fear. However, when Dr Wallace came out of her office to greet me, I felt immediately at ease. She was young, but not too young, and she had a kind smile and a gentle voice. She was one of those people who looked soft but held herself with a confidence that made you feel like you were in safe hands.

In my experience, the first session with a psychologist is always the hardest. You only have 45 minutes to figure each other out and decide if this is something that might work long-term. You attempt to give an accurate run-down of how fucked up your mind is, while trying to hold it together. But you also want the psychologist to give you enough of an idea about who *they* are and why they're the right person to treat you. It's like the worst speed-dating experience of your life, but it feels like the stakes are higher—and you're guaranteed to cry. I'd always leave my first sessions feeling raw and unbearably exposed.

I tried not to pin all my hopes on my first session with Dr Wallace, but deep down I knew that if it didn't go well, I'd feel completely dejected. Thankfully, I left the session feeling confident that she was the one to carry me across the abyss of OCD and into greener pastures.

Dr Wallace confidently diagnosed me with OCD during our first session. This wasn't a surprise to me; I'd diagnosed myself years before when I'd read the magazine article written by my anonymous saviour. But having a professional diagnosis felt affirming. Dr Wallace did something for me in those first 45 minutes that I'd been craving for most of my life: she validated my experience and told me that none of it was my fault. I had a mental illness, which can be devastating, but which is also very responsive to treatment. It was a line in the sand, and from here I'd do everything within my power to fight the beast that had been controlling my mind and my happiness since I was six.

And the best thing was that I no longer felt alone in this fight.

WHY A DIAGNOSIS CAN BE SO IMPORTANT

Receiving a diagnosis is a privilege that not all people with mental illness currently enjoy. It means having the time and money to see several different healthcare professionals. Ideally, those who need it will have access to a Mental Health Treatment Plan, which subsidises the cost of ten sessions a year with a psychologist or allied mental health professional. However, in a post-Covid-19 world, the system is clearly buckling under pressure, and not everyone is able to access the help they need. For more information about what to do while you're waiting for help, turn to Chapter 7.

If you're able to find a mental health professional and receive a diagnosis, it can be life-changing. It can offer hope and a sense that there's light at the end of a long, dark tunnel. Clinical psychologist Dr Victoria Miller, Associate Director of the Melbourne Wellbeing Group, witnesses a multitude of emotions in her clients when they receive an OCD diagnosis.

'Getting a diagnosis can really normalise what's happening for them. I think it's a sense of universality that connects them to other people in the world who are going through the same thing. So, people feel less alone,' says Dr Miller.

Of course, not everyone will feel positive feelings when they are diagnosed. For some it feels scary to have a name or label stuck to them. It can feel oppressive or perhaps even embarrassing. There is still so much misunderstanding when it comes to OCD, and some people may not feel comfortable disclosing their diagnosis to others.

However, a diagnosis often means gaining access to treatment. Dr Miller calls a diagnosis your 'golden ticket to treatment'.

'I also think it gives them a framework to understand themselves. I think it gives them a road map for recovery,' she explains.

For me, it truly felt like a new world opening up, especially once I started exposure and response prevention (ERP). There was a way out of the maze. I'm still unsure if I've found the exit, but I've gotten closer, and even *knowing* there's an exit gives me so much hope, where before I only had despair.

I haven't found that treatment is a linear process, whereby I've become symptom-free after a certain number of sessions. This may be the case with some people, but for many it's a more unpredictable work in progress. But the more I learn about OCD, the more ammunition I have against it.

DOING HARD THINGS

If Dr Andrea Wallace ever asked me to jump off a cliff, I'd probably consider it. Because she's asked things of me that have felt scarier than jumping off a cliff, and I've survived. Dr Wallace uses ERP therapy when treating her clients with OCD. I'd read about ERP in the six months I was on her waiting list. The concept scared the shit out of me, because it totally contradicted all my years of 'just trying to let the thought go'. But here I was, a 31-year-old who had been tormented by OCD since the age of six, and I'd gotten nowhere with positive thinking or thought suppression. I was at a crossroads, and I could choose the familiar path—which would lead to a lifetime of shutting myself away to think my way out of my obsessions—or trek up the treacherous mountain and fling myself off into my sea of fears.

I'm convinced that whenever we choose to do hard things, it's often for other people rather than ourselves. I could probably have gone through life letting myself down on the many occasions when OCD would completely ravage me. What I couldn't comprehend was the thought of letting my child down. It reminds me of a quote from the book *All That I Am* by Anna Funder: 'One does not remember one's own pain. It is the suffering of others that undoes us.'[1]

I didn't want to be a mentally unwell mother; I wanted to be a positive, stable presence in Benji's life. To achieve this, I'd need to try the treatment that had so many experts endorsing it.

WHAT IS ERP?

Exposure and response prevention (ERP) is a type of cognitive behavioural therapy (CBT). To understand how ERP plays such an important role in the treatment of OCD, we first need to understand what CBT is.

Cognitive therapy (the C in CBT) is about challenging unhelpful thought patterns or emotional responses. Behavioural therapy (the B in CBT) is about changing behaviours that are causing the person to experience more anxiety and stress. There are different kinds of behavioural therapies, but the one that I'm going to focus on is ERP.

ERP comprises two parts: exposure, which involves facing the thoughts, images, objects or situations that activate your obsessions; and response prevention, which is choosing not to carry out the compulsion you perform when you're triggered.[2] While this can sound scary, over time—if you expose yourself to your fear and then stop yourself from carrying out your compulsion—you'll see a decline in your anxiety level, and this is called habituation.[3]

It's essential to acknowledge the difference between exposure therapy for a phobia, such as flying, and ERP for OCD. For a phobia, the idea is that if you expose yourself enough times to a particular fear, over time it will lessen. However, to reduce the symptoms of OCD, you must add the *second* step, which is trying to stop yourself from engaging in your compulsive behaviour.

Dr Andrea Wallace stresses the importance of that second step for anyone who has OCD.

'Sometimes people can get a bit confused by that and feel like they're doing exposure just by putting themselves in a situation where their intrusive thoughts get triggered. But if they're not dropping their compulsions, all they're doing is terrorising themselves, because their distress is being triggered, and the meaning that they have assigned to their thoughts (e.g., I am in danger, I am bad) continues to be reinforced by their performance of compulsions,' she says.

This can be particularly difficult when your compulsion involves mental rituals such as mental checking, replaying events in your mind or trying to neutralise distressing images.

These behaviours can be a little trickier to 'catch out', and sometimes you'll do them without even realising it.

The research

ERP is often described as the 'gold standard' of treatment for OCD. There have been numerous studies assessing its effectiveness. The American Psychological Association and the American Psychiatric Association both recommend ERP, the latter noting that it has the best evidentiary support.[4] Esteemed psychologist Professor Jonathan Abramowitz has called ERP 'one of the great success stories within the field of mental health'.[5]

Research suggests that 70 per cent of people with OCD will benefit significantly from using ERP.[6] It has been recommended that around fifteen to twenty treatment sessions are needed for best results, and that weekly (or more intensive) sessions are optimal.[7]

IS YOUR THERAPIST TRAINED TO DO ERP?

Unfortunately, there's no official training that therapists must complete to be able to carry out ERP with clients. Training and mentoring do exist, but they're not mandatory.

Dr Andrea Wallace's advice is to make sure that your therapist is actively trying to investigate the base fear that triggers your obsessions.

'I would be keeping an eye on whether they're asking you enough questions about your compulsions, and whether they're asking about the fear that underlies the intrusive thought.

For example, it may be that you have an intrusive thought— *maybe I'm going to harm my baby*—but what's terrifying is not that intrusive thought, because there's such a large part of you that knows deep down you're not going to do that. But the idea that this intrusive thought might horrify your partner so much that they would leave you could be the root fear,' she explains.

'The compulsion might be to seek reassurance from your partner that you are a good and lovable person. So, you need someone who's prepared to dig with you to get to where the scary bit is, so you can then make sure that you can match the exposure to that feared outcome. You don't need someone who might think, *Well, this person is actually afraid that they're going to hurt their baby*. Because that's not really the point— the point is that the therapist needs to stop you from seeking reassurance from your partner,' Dr Wallace continues.

CREATING AN EXPOSURE HIERARCHY

One way that therapists approach ERP with their clients is to create an exposure hierarchy. This is a pyramid that lists all of the ways that a person's obsessions could be triggered—in order of least distressing at the bottom to most distressing at the top. With her clients, Dr Andrea Wallace likes to put a percentage next to each trigger (100 per cent being the most difficult).

'Once we've made the list and we've rated the situations from the least triggering to the most triggering, we then want to enter the process at about 40 per cent, because if we can have a win straight off the bat, the person will get some confidence and think, *Oh my goodness, I'll be able to find my way out of this*,' she explains.

For someone who is fearful of becoming contaminated with a disease, one of the triggers identified in an exposure hierarchy could be touching the inside of a bin. This fear might sit at 50 per cent on their scale of distress, so Dr Wallace would encourage the person to find a bin with her (during the session) and put their hands inside the bin. This is the exposure. The response prevention part would then be to avoid washing their hands, and to sit with the discomfort of the questions arising in their mind (for example, *What if I get sick? What if I then pass that sickness on to someone else?*).

A trigger higher up on the pyramid might be touching the bin and then licking their hands. So, Dr Wallace would perform this exposure with her client, and then she would encourage them to sit with the distress that is bubbling up, without running to the bathroom to wash their hands and mouth. Instead of trying to convince them that they won't get sick, she would encourage them to think, *Maybe I will get sick. Perhaps by not washing off the germs, I will contract a disease. I might, I might not, I don't know, and it's safe not to know.*

An example of an exposure for a mental compulsion could be to record a 'loop tape' on a phone, where the client verbalises their fears, and then have them listen to it repeatedly.

For someone who is afraid that they might be attracted to somebody other than their partner, Dr Wallace might ask them to look up other people on the internet whom they find attractive. They might start scanning their body to make sure that they're not experiencing a feeling of arousal. (This is the mental compulsion). She would then encourage them to make a voice recording saying something like: 'Maybe I do have feelings of arousal. Maybe I'm more attracted to this person, and maybe that means I will leave my partner and try to pursue this person. I don't know for certain.'

'We're undoing the mental ritual. So, if the habit has provided reassurance that they're safe in their relationship, then we want to undo this habit. Because without erasing that mental ritual, they're still providing themselves with safety through using the compulsions, which means that they will still be invested in the thought as being *important* or *meaningful*. Basically, we want to treat thoughts as being completely meaningless,' explains Dr Wallace.

'One of the things I hear clients say a lot are the words "really close". So, people will say, "I think I'm *really close* to leaving my partner. So, this must mean that I am leaving my partner." So, I ask them, "Is the car packed? Have you walked out the door yet?" And if you haven't, then you haven't left them. You're still in the game.

'We cannot equate a big urge or a big feeling with an action. They're very distinct. One of the most important things to learn is that our thoughts do not magically turn into the behaviour. Even when we feel like we've got really close to something. If it hasn't happened, it hasn't happened,' she explains with a sparkle in her eyes.

For clients who have Harm OCD, and who might be afraid of hurting someone with a knife, Dr Wallace has brought a knife into her sessions and encouraged them to hold it up to her throat. It may sound extreme, but getting them to perform this kind of exposure is often a huge turning point for them (and just another day in the office for her).

'People don't do it. They don't actually go through with it. I haven't been stabbed yet,' Dr Wallace says with a wide smile. Have I mentioned that nothing fazes this woman?

'It's a really liberating experience, because people are afraid that their thoughts will turn into action. That the urge means something. But it doesn't mean anything. And it's such a relief for them to realise this,' she says.

WHAT IF ERP ISN'T WORKING?

In Dr Andrea Wallace's experience, if ERP isn't working for someone, it's generally because there's something that's stopping them from completely letting go of their compulsions. And when the compulsions are maintained, the anxiety stubbornly hangs around—or possibly gets worse.

'Compulsions are the air that OCD breathes. If you take away the compulsions, the OCD falls apart. It can't keep itself together. It just can't hold,' she says.

Someone might be continuing to engage in their compulsions because they haven't properly teased apart their obsessions and compulsions. Or it could be because they simply aren't ready to let them go.

'I've learned how important it is to always meet a client where they're at. So even though they've come along, saying that they want to do ERP, what they're really wanting at that point is validation and understanding. They need somebody in the world who gets them while they continue to engage in compulsions,' says Dr Wallace with a shrug.

Another obstacle that could be getting in the way is that they have started the process too high up on the hierarchy. People need early 'wins' to stay motivated. If the initial distress is so high that it overwhelms them, they won't give the treatment method a chance to work.

MEDICATION AND ERP

OCD is both biological and learned, which is why a two-pronged approach—taking medication and doing ERP therapy—is often thought to be a good option. Dr Jonathan Grayson explains this beautifully in *Freedom from Obsessive-Compulsive Disorder*.

'When medication is needed, it is because something is biologically wrong that no amount of strength and fortitude will change. And it is not a panacea, because it will only affect the biological components of your OCD. Medication doesn't make you forget how to add, or whom you feel love for, and it doesn't undo all the OCD learning that has taken place.'[8]

Medication can often allow people with OCD to get to a point where they feel strong enough to start therapy and work on the obsessive triggers that have been learned. They can then work towards becoming symptom-free over time.

Dr Scott Blair-West agrees. Even though a large part of his job as a psychiatrist is prescribing medication, he is also a big proponent of ERP.

'Although people come and see me for OCD, and they often want information about the pills, I normally tell them that pills are about a third of what is going to help you, and exposure is the other two thirds.'

FIGHTING THE URGE

My first foray into ERP was to record a loop tape. At the time—once again—I was stuck with obsessions about sexual orientation. I still had never felt like I wanted to be in a relationship with a woman or had any urge to engage in any sexual activity with a woman, but because I'd never faced these thoughts head-on, they still caused me distress. I need to reiterate that the actual fear—once Dr Andrea Wallace helped me realise it—wasn't being gay. It was that if I realised I *was* gay, then I'd have to break up my family. Dr Wallace and I created my exposure hierarchy. Sitting at the base of the pyramid was recording a loop tape, and at the top was watching lesbian porn. Wedged in the middle were activities such as listening to sex-related podcasts, reading articles about women who had left their male partners for women, and watching TV shows with explicit sex scenes. So, we started with the loop tape.

The idea of the loop tape is to record yourself saying the things you're most fearful of, and then listening to that recording repeatedly without performing compulsions. One of the most uncomfortable parts of this whole experience was recording the tape in front of Dr Wallace. Saying my fears out loud was hard enough, but recording them into the microphone on my iPhone was torture. The loop tape went something like this: 'Maybe I have always been gay, and I have never been attracted to men. Maybe I will realise I'm gay, and I will have to leave Hugh and break up my family. Perhaps I'll walk out one day, and everyone will be angry and disappointed in me.'

Once I'd recorded the tape, Dr Wallace asked me to immediately listen to it. I'd been squirming throughout the whole session, but this request almost sent me over the edge. 'I can't!' I blurted out.

'Why not?' she asked, looking genuinely confused.

'It's just so embarrassing,' I said, shifting uncomfortably in my chair. I desperately wanted time to speed up so this session could be over, and I could race to my car and drive off into the sunset.

But Dr Wallace wasn't the slightest bit embarrassed or uncomfortable. She assured me that she'd heard it all before. She almost looked bored. The woman was completely unflappable.

'This is all part of it. If you want to get better, you must learn to be uncomfortable. You need to dive right in, trusting that it will work,' she explained.

'Fuck it,' I groaned. I wanted to get better. Fear and embarrassment had gotten me nowhere so far. It was time to get uncomfortable.

I hated the sound of my own voice, but I hit the 'play' button and heard my nervous voice articulate my obsessive thoughts, which I was so used to hearing in my own head but never out loud. It wasn't a pleasant experience—and listening to it made my heart race and my palms sweat—but I did it.

'Great,' said Dr Wallace. 'Now just listen to it multiple times a day. Whenever you get a spare moment—walking to the train station, on the train, walking from the station to your office, in your lunch break, after work, before bed. As many times as you can in a day.'

What the FUCK have I got myself into? I wondered as I trudged out of her office and back to my car.

Always the diligent student who didn't like to let her teacher down, I listened to that tape over and over for the next week. At first, I'd grind my teeth and clench my fists while listening. But by the 30th or 40th time, it barely caused me to flinch. When I could listen to it and have my mind wander off to some other topic, I knew that we would be advancing to a higher level of the pyramid in our next session.

My next ERP task was to listen to any kind of podcast on the topic of sex. One of the ways my compulsions would play out was trying to avoid any kind of material on the topic of sex, whether it was books, movies or TV shows. It wasn't that I didn't enjoy sex, it was that if I was exposed to anything sexually explicit, my mind would always try to find a way to bring up my obsessive thoughts around sexuality. So, throughout the years, while everyone was obsessing over *Sex and the City*, *Girls* and *Orange is the New Black*, I was much more likely to be watching some tame British drama or comedy that wouldn't provoke any obsessions.

According to Dr Wallace, this avoidance needed to stop, because it was placing importance on the fears and only making them bigger and scarier as a result. So, under her instructions, I started to download podcasts such as *The Hook Up*, *Call Her Daddy* and Abbie Chatfield's *It's A Lot*. Any time I was driving in the car or walking the dog, I pressed play on my phone, and I'd tune in to topics that ranged from threesomes and anal to ethical non-monogamy and infidelity. Just like with the loop tape, at the beginning of my foray into this explicit world my whole body would tense up; if I was walking, then I'd speed up so I could get home and turn off the podcast. However, after about three weeks of listening to almost every sex-related podcast I could find, there was very little that shocked me. Clit talk? Meh. A finger in the bum to make you cum? Boring!

Of course, at times I did feel the anxiety ramp up, and as a result I'd start treading the well-worn path of rumination. But Dr Wallace's voice would echo in my head, and I'd try my hardest to stop the cycle and sit (or walk) with the uneasiness until it passed, or at least lessened. Knowing that I had a session coming up with Dr Wallace where I'd be held accountable for my actions—thanks to her question, 'How did you go with your exposure?'—spurred me to keep at it, even when it felt unbearable.

Over the next few months, I made my way to the top of the hierarchy. Whenever I had a moment to myself and no one was around, I'd have to watch all kinds of porn or look at pornographic imagery and then sit with any discomfort that would arise. This is no easy feat with a tiny person running around (especially a tiny person who barely slept a wink until he was three). 'Darling, please shut your eyes so Mummy can go and watch some hardcore porn that will push her to the brink of an anxiety attack.'

Trust me, I know how odd this all sounds, but I was trying to normalise something to which I'd attached so much fear over the years. As soon as I noticed myself performing a compulsion—whether it was trying to think about all the reasons why I wasn't gay, or replaying sexual experiences in my mind—I'd have to say to myself, 'Well, maybe I am gay. Maybe I don't want to be with men, and I'll have to leave my family. I'm not sure, no one can ever be 100 per cent sure.' And as inconvenient and uncomfortable as this activity was, over time I noticed a huge shift in my obsessions and compulsions. The frenetic looping thoughts slowed down, and the panic that accompanied them lessened. I was starting to experience habituation: realising that I wasn't in any danger, and that nothing bad would happen if I didn't perform my compulsions.

Another example of ERP I did with Dr Wallace was trying to tackle my panic disorder. Ever since my teenage years, I'd experience periods when I felt like I couldn't get enough oxygen into my body. I'd try to take quicker and deeper breaths, but this would just lead to hyperventilation. I'd never actually pass out, but I'd feel like I was constantly on the verge of losing consciousness. Often it would happen when I wasn't even aware that I was feeling anxious. It was like my body was sounding an alarm before the intruder had even arrived. I'd usually spend the next few days convinced that I'd pass out or die, while trying to go about my life as usual. A few times I tried to explain the experience to family and friends, which resulted in a sympathetic comment or two. But no one really knew what to say. They knew that I wasn't going to die; nothing was wrong with my heart. 'Just keep breathing,' someone said at some point. Cool. Thanks.

I decided to bring up this problem with Dr Wallace during one of Melbourne's trillion lockdowns in 2020. Compared to so many others, I hadn't suffered much throughout the pandemic: I remained healthy, I didn't know anyone who had lost their life to Covid-19, Hugh was able to continue working, and I had plenty of family and friends within the 5-kilometre travel zone whom I could see during the repetitive days, which all seemed to blur into one. I was extremely lucky and am very aware of that. However, like so many other parents and carers I know, the lockdowns took their toll. I had given birth to our second child, Elsie, about six weeks before the pandemic hit, so being stuck at home with a baby and a toddler for months on end was exhausting, to put it mildly. Benji and I seemed to be locked in an eternal battle of wills throughout the day, and before Hugh could even get his key into the lock, I was sprinting out the door with the dog, getting some 'fresh air' all the way to the bottle shop so I could stockpile some more shiraz. Mercifully, my obsessions remained relatively dormant during the first few months of Elsie's life (most likely because I was still doing regular therapy) but the panicked breathing set in often, and would last for days on end. It probably had something to do with the incessant news scrolling I'd do throughout the days and nights, searching for some glimmer of hope among the bleak warnings and depressing headlines.

When I brought up the breathing issue with Dr Wallace, she nodded her head like she knew this would come up at some point. I thought she'd ask me to do some calming breathing exercises, but I should have known that she wasn't this predictable.

'Okay, what you need to do when you feel like your breaths are getting short is to take even shorter breaths,' she said.

'What? No . . . you don't understand. I'll pass out if I do that,' I explained.

'Yeah, you might. But you probably won't. You need to start trusting that your body knows how to breathe. It's been doing it a long time, and you're trying to control a system that already works perfectly.'

As soon as the telehealth appointment ended, and Dr Wallace's comforting face disappeared from my screen, I felt the urge to take in more air.

'Fight the urge,' I heard her voice echo in my head.

So, I went against every instinct and took shorter, quicker breaths. I did it for about twenty seconds at a time. It felt like torture at the beginning, and I kept grabbing at my desk in case I started to pass out—but I never lost consciousness. I now realise that I was never going to. After about three days of trying to make myself hyperventilate, the urge to get more oxygen into my lungs decreased. Like all of the ERP therapies I've done, it felt unbelievably uncomfortable and counterintuitive, but it worked.

Dr Andrea Wallace: The Lion metaphor

Dr Wallace used the Lion metaphor with me in one of our sessions. It's something that I've found to be helpful to think about when I'm struggling to resist compulsions. I hope you also find it helpful.

Try to conceptualise your anxiety as a lion. The lion starts as a little cub, and each time it roars, you experience the symptoms of anxiety—your heart rate quickens, your chest gets tight, you might start sweating. The lion roars when you come across some uncertainty, and in this moment you have a choice: either starve the lion or feed the lion. The lion feeds on avoidance, and in the case of OCD this avoidance comes in the form of compulsions. So, when you perform a compulsion, you'll get a sense of relief. The lion is now silent because it's munching away on the avoidance. But because you've just fed it, it will become bigger and stronger. The next time you come across the uncertainty, the lion will roar again, but it will be louder this time. Your anxiety symptoms are even more intense.

But you have another choice: starve the lion. If you choose to sit with the uncertainty, then you starve it of avoidance. The lion becomes angry, because it's used to being fed—so it will roar and roar, and you might feel bone-shaking anxiety as it roars. But the lion will eventually roar itself hoarse and quieten down. Because you haven't fed the lion, the next time you come across the uncertainty, the lion is smaller, and it won't be so loud. Eventually, as you starve the lion, it will become so small and meek that you'll barely hear it.

Chapter 9

ROCD AND ME

Hugh and I became engaged about six months prior to my first session with clinical psychologist Dr Andrea Wallace. The pressure of an upcoming wedding had me in a spin. I was deeply in love with Hugh, but my OCD was making me question whether I loved him *enough*. And how do you ever know if you love someone enough to spend the rest of your life with them? How do you measure your love and your feelings of certainty?

The short answer is that you can't. You need to trust your feelings and hope for the best. But for someone with OCD, trusting yourself is just about the hardest thing you can do. I hadn't been able to trust myself or my thoughts since I was a little girl, because I never knew what was fact and what was fiction. It wasn't until I started therapy with Dr Wallace that I realised what I was experiencing (and had experienced in the past with other partners) was Relationship OCD (ROCD).

RELATIONSHIP OCD (ROCD)

This is a theme of OCD that revolves around intimate relationships. I'll be referring to ROCD in the context of romantic partners, but it can also manifest with other relationships such as a parent–child relationship. ROCD can affect anyone, regardless of whether you're male, female or non-binary.

The anxiety induced by ROCD often leads to compulsions such as reassurance-seeking, ruminating and avoidance. Sometimes relationships suffer enormously, because it can be hard for people with OCD to distinguish between OCD symptoms and reality.

PARTNER-FOCUSED AND RELATIONSHIP-FOCUSED ROCD

Partner-focused ROCD tends to revolve around your partner's perceived flaws. Common partner-focused obsessions include:

- fixating on physical features (for example, *their nose is too big*)
- focusing on social or personality attributes (for example, *they're not outgoing enough*; *they aren't ambitious enough*)
- comparing the current partner with past relationships (for example, *was I more attracted to my ex? Did my partner love their ex more than they love me?*).

Relationship-focused ROCD centres more on the overall quality of the relationship or the feelings you have towards your partner (or they might have about you). Common relationship-focused obsessions include:

- If I'm not feeling in love all the time, how do I know that they are the one for me?
- Do I feel aroused during sex?
- What if I cheated on my partner, but I can't remember?

WHY DOES IT HAPPEN?

There's no way around it: relationships are complicated beasts. And because romantic love is so tied up with Western cultural obsessions about 'the one', it's easy to fall into the trap of wondering if what we're feeling is *right* or *enough*. There's so much pressure to feel butterflies in our stomach, to fall giddily in love and to settle down with 'the one', our soulmate. We must be head over heels in love, feel sparks and see fireworks, but at the same time we need to find the person who makes us feel comfortable and safe. From a young age, we're sold the dream that all of these contradictory feelings are attainable—and that *we'll just know* when we've found the Yin to our Yang.

In reality, however, relationships are often hard work. They can be exciting and fulfilling, but they can also be tiresome and dull, and even the best relationship can be unpleasant at times.

Everyone will face doubt in their relationships—this is just a fact of life. However, if your thoughts start to cause significant distress, you're spending large amounts of time trying to 'work out' whether your relationship is right, or your obsessions start to negatively affect your relationship or other areas of your life, then it's worth seeking help.

ROCD is often triggered by life events that call for significant commitment, such as engagements, weddings and having kids. Cruelly, ROCD is likely to show up when we've found someone we feel genuinely happy with and would be scared to lose (remember, OCD thoughts are ego-dystonic, meaning they are out of step with our values).

As Sheva Rajaee, author of *Relationship OCD*, says, 'ROCD doesn't show up in just any relationship; it shows up in good ones, ones with lasting power, ones that might actually be worth doing the work for.'[1]

WHAT'S THE DIFFERENCE BETWEEN ROCD AND GENUINE RELATIONSHIP DOUBTS?

Looking back on past relationships, it's now clear to me when I was feeling genuine doubt about compatibility and when I was besieged with ROCD fears. However, at the time it was hard to trust myself enough to know the difference.

When I ask Sheva Rajaee about this, she says it's important to recognise when doubts become disproportionate to the real safety in the relationship.

'A partner who is good, kind and loving causing a feeling of repulsion or terror doesn't quite add up. But the truth is that there is no clear difference between routine doubts and ROCD;

rather, it is more like a blend. Often, an honest incompatibility in the relationship—say, difference in sexual desire—can become caught in the OCD web and spun into a catastrophe, when differences between people are part of all relationships and must be managed. The goal of ROCD work is to correct the disproportionate response, not to eliminate the trigger,' she explains.

TREATMENT

ROCD is generally treated with the same approaches as other forms of OCD. Exposure and response prevention (ERP) is used to habituate sufferers with uncertainty, so they become comfortable with *not knowing* and subsequently break the vicious OCD cycle. Some examples of treating ROCD with ERP include watching a romantic movie and then avoiding the compulsion to compare your relationship with the one on the screen, or spending time with your partner and later stopping yourself from asking friends or family members if they think that your partner is the 'right' one for you. Over time, by purposefully triggering your obsessions, you'll realise that you can tolerate uncertainty when it comes to relationships, and you can sit in that grey area where there are no absolutes—because that's where everyone sits, whether or not they have OCD and despite how 'perfect' their relationship seems.

When you have ROCD, you're generally dealing with fear-based 'faulty thinking', so it can be beneficial to challenge your thoughts and any rules you've created for yourself, on top of using ERP. Consequently, in addition to ERP, other forms of therapy—such as acceptance and commitment therapy (ACT) and more general cognitive behavioural therapy (CBT)—can be useful.

Because ROCD can take such a toll on a relationship, Sheva Rajaee, who treats people with OCD on a day-to-day basis at her clinic in California, recommends bringing your partner along to therapy for a session, especially if the therapist has experience with OCD.

'Even giving them time to speak to the therapist alone can be really useful, so they may ask sensitive questions the sufferer might not want to hear. It's important that the partner also understands the difference between supportive statements [*I can see this is really hard for you*] and reassurance-giving statements [*Of course we're perfect together!*],' she explains.

One of the most helpful things I ever did was to bring Hugh in for a session with my psychologist, Dr Andrea Wallace, so she could articulate to him what I was experiencing. Both Hugh and I have found our conversations with Dr Wallace about ROCD extremely helpful. In fact, that's an understatement: they've completely changed the way I look at relationships and made me feel much more secure and content in my relationship. We spend so much of our lives trying to build and maintain connections with others, but we're rarely taught practical information to help us to navigate the inevitable ups and downs that accompany relationships.

Dr Andrea Wallace: Doubt and the 'myth of the one'

In this box I thought I'd share some of Dr Wallace's wisdom in case you're experiencing ROCD and looking for help.

Doubt is not normalised in society. You're supposed to find *the one*, and you're supposed to have no doubt about it. And it's just appalling. It leaves people feeling trapped. Because if there's this idea out there in the world that you're supposed to be gloriously happy in every moment and aroused at every second, then it creates this ridiculous standard for our feeling space, which is completely unreliable, changeable and beautifully messy.

Love as an action

We often code love as a feeling rather than an action. Telling yourself the following can be helpful.

Regardless of what's going through my mind or body in this moment, I choose to:

- *be as kind as I can*
- *be as present as I can*
- *put up with you*
- *not walk out the door.*

We must shift away from love as a feeling and move towards love as a choice that we make repeatedly. There's such beauty in a love that's chosen in the moments when you're like, *You're annoying the hell out of me right now. And I'm choosing to stay through gritted teeth.* The glory of that kind of love! Where is that in the love songs?

Normalisation and anxiety

When working with someone experiencing ROCD, I will typically step in with some kind of normalisation. I'll remind my clients that we are all in doubt. Often we'll all find our partners icky and we'll all experience really shit sex, or not be attracted to other people, and just being able to normalise that for people is helpful.

Sometimes I will talk about my own experience of having bone-shaking doubt. And one of the things that I will talk about is the experience of when we are afraid of our feelings. The fear of the feelings will trigger anxiety, and the experience of anxiety will overshadow all other kinds of tender feelings. Anxiety is a trigger to help us to survive, and it was created at a time when survival required us to be able to fight or get the hell out of there. The sympathetic nervous system will make sure that we are entirely focused on the thing that we're afraid of.

If our mind thinks that we are in danger, it will not give us access to desire. Anxiety is like a fire blanket: it will put out all other feelings. So, if we require that our feelings only be sweetness and desire and passion, or arousal and interest and curiosity, then the demand will freak the crap out of us and will trigger our anxiety, and we will not be able to find those tender feelings.

At the end of the day, we must treat our feelings as if they are problematic data, so that we stop relying upon them. Even if you've thought about all the different ways you would pack the car and where you would go to stay [when you leave your partner], it's just not the same as walking out the door. And it's very important to be able to go, *Ah okay. Thinking about walking out the door is not walking out the door. There's a difference.*

My relationship with Hugh is not perfect—no relationship is, no matter how glossy it looks from the outside. But learning about ROCD has led me to expect and embrace the imperfections.

Emma's story

When Emma found herself scrambling through a bin at her hotel in Bali, trying to find a tampon she had used the night before to be 100 per cent certain she couldn't have cheated on her partner (with whom she was very much in love), she knew that she had probably hit her lowest moment in her OCD nightmare.

But I'll rewind for some context.

When Emma was at the tender age of six, her mum passed away from breast cancer. It was around this time that her OCD was first triggered.

Understandably, she was terrified that her dad would also die, so she would perform physical compulsions—such as tapping things a certain number of times, closing doors in a certain way or putting things in certain spots—to convince herself that she was helping to keep him safe.

After a few years, these compulsions seemed to disappear. However, when she was 21 and about to move to Perth by herself, her OCD was once again triggered. Emma had gone to see a clairvoyant with a friend, and as soon as she left, she felt panicked that she'd ruined her life by finding out everything that was going to happen.

'I was just constantly panicking about how I'd ruined my life. [I felt as if] there was no mystery, because she'd just foretold everything. But I would apply it to all these different things, like if I dated someone, I'd end up hysterically crying and thinking, *Well, there's no point in me dating them, because they're not "the one"; I'm not the age that she said I would be when I met "the one"*. I would just be at this sort of extreme level of panic all the time,' explains Emma.

Emma is like a walking, talking ray of sunshine. With a huge smile, sparkling eyes and a warmth that makes you feel like you're basking by a fire, it's hard to imagine her in a state of panic. But I've come to realise that you can rarely pick those with OCD from the outside. In fact, most of the time it's those you least suspect who are suffering the most.

Emma went to see a counsellor at her university, but her OCD wasn't picked up. It wasn't until a fear of HIV came along that the clairvoyant panic was replaced.

'I think it was the fact that HIV was one of the only STIs [sexually transmissible infections] I knew about that was incurable. And, I had two uncles who passed away from AIDS on my mum's side. I think it was kind of on my mind, so the thought would sometimes be: *What if I pricked myself on something and now I have HIV?*'

Emma started worrying that if she went out drinking, then she wouldn't remember everything that happened. She convinced herself that she had probably slept with someone, completely blanked it out and was now infected with HIV. When she read that HIV could only be picked up in a blood test three months after the potential exposure, she would live those months as if she was infected and was going to die.

'By the time I'd get a blood test, I'd be shocked when it came back negative. I had so many blood tests! I started doctor shopping, because my doctor stopped doing them. She was like, "I'm not giving you another blood test for HIV." So, I'd go to a different doctor to get a pathology form,' says Emma.

A new obsession

When Emma met her partner, Adam, she knew that she had finally found someone she felt invested in. So, of course, the obsessions morphed into something that was now more relevant to her situation. If she went out and had a few drinks, instead of worrying about contracting HIV, she started to wonder whether she'd kissed someone else but couldn't remember.

'It was like, *Oh my God, this is the new thing you care about*,' says Emma, dread still visible in her eyes when she talks about the onset of this particular obsession.

To calm her anxiety after a night out, she would seek reassurance from the friends who had been with her. She would ask them to account for all of her movements throughout the night, so she could meticulously piece together the evening and rule out any possible drunken dalliance with someone who wasn't her partner.

Eventually, the distress got so bad that she started contacting the people with whom she was convinced 'something' had happened.

'I called a guy who I was dancing with at a work ball, because I was worried that maybe I'd kissed him. It took me a few weeks to build up the courage to do it. I called him and was like, "Hey, just wondering, was I inappropriate towards you?"

'He was like, "Yeah, really, no. You were on your best behaviour. You didn't do anything; you have nothing to worry about."'

But the relief didn't last long.

'Pretty much as soon as I made that call, I was like, *Yeah, but he was really drunk, so maybe he doesn't remember? Maybe he's just covering his tracks by not telling me what really happened?* So, yeah, it was exhausting.'

After a couple of years, the obsession resurfaced, and Emma started panicking again about any possible indiscretions on the dance floor that she had blanked out. She needed certainty but had already talked to everyone she could think of who was there. So, she decided to find out if there was footage from the venue.

'I started calling the club and ... Okay, this is embarrassing, but I tried pretending to be all these different people to try to get footage. I was like, "I'm calling from HR at blah blah company." And I was like, "I just wonder whether you keep footage that long?" And they said that they thought they had it, but I'd need a warrant to get it. And I genuinely started to think, *How can I get a warrant*?'

But when Emma found out that they had, in fact, destroyed the footage, she was gutted. She now felt like she would always be tortured by the uncertainty. She knew that she couldn't handle much more of this.

Which brings us back to the bin in Bali. Since Emma felt as if she couldn't trust her own memory, she started wearing a tampon when she went out. She was using the logic that at the end of the night she could take it out, safe in the knowledge that she couldn't have had sex with anyone else. Sometimes this would help, but obsessions are like the Terminator: they're never down for long.

'This night in Bali, I'd clearly had a shower when I got home, and taken out the tampon. But then in the morning, I suddenly started doubting my memory and was like, *Did I take it out? I can't remember.*

'It's those extreme moments when you're like, *What am I doing? What has it come to?* I'm going through a bin, looking for a tampon that I've used, to make sure that I haven't ...' Emma trails off, still incredulous at the power her obsessions had over her.

Diagnosis and therapy

Luckily, Emma soon came across STOP Therapy at Swinburne University, and realised that her symptoms were similar to those listed on the website. She was diagnosed with OCD and then introduced to ERP in a group-therapy setting. She started medication after seeing a general practitioner (GP), and the obsessions and compulsions slowly started to die down.

Over the years, Emma had stopped drinking when she went out, or she would rigidly stop at one so that she could rely on her memory. So, one of her first exposures was going out and having three or more drinks. Higher up on her exposure hierarchy was having three or more drinks by herself and then getting an Uber home, because then she couldn't rely on anyone else to reassure her that nothing had happened.

'Whenever I was alone and couldn't check with someone else exactly where I'd been or what I'd done, I didn't trust my own memory. So, I'd be like, *What if I cheated with the Uber driver in the Uber on the way home?*' Emma explains.

But slowly she learned how to sit with the discomfort of not knowing. Of course, she could always make a pretty good guess about what had happened. Logically, she knew that she was staying faithful, but OCD doesn't do logic.

With her psychologist, Emma realised that her obsessions were springing from a deeper place of not feeling worthy of love. Not being worthy of joy and happiness.

'Through therapy, I became more aware that I needed to start living as though I was deserving of love. And I had to stop putting things on hold until I was better,' she says.

Although there have been low moments when Emma thought it would be easier to resign herself to a solitary life, where she wouldn't ever have to worry about hurting anyone or ruining anything, she and Adam are still together. Emma has always been able to talk about her obsessions with Adam, which has made things so much easier for her.

'He really does quite deeply understand it, and understands not to provide reassurance, but it's uncomfortable if I'm sitting with uncertainty. If we've been out and had some drinks, the next morning he'll check in with me and be like, "Do you need anything? Is it a pretty tough day today?" That sort of stuff. He's really been incredibly understanding and never, ever judgemental about it, which has been so special,' says Emma.

Chapter 10

THE REVELATION
AND THE RELAPSE

During one of my sessions with Dr Andrea Wallace, she put forward a proposal: 'I want to set up an obsessive-compulsive disorder group-therapy session with four other people I treat.'

Just the thought of having to share my obsessions with other people made me feel ill. However, being a compliant patient, my response didn't reflect my inner turmoil at all.

'Cool. That would probably be really helpful,' I said with a forced smile.

'Excellent. You'll love them. They're all beautiful, compassionate, successful people who have had a similar experience with OCD as you. What I hope is that you see yourself in them and realise that you, too, are a lovable person,' she said, genuinely excited about the prospect of this idea working.

But the idea of seeing four other versions of myself sitting on uncomfortable chairs in a windowless room, staring back at me, made me sick to my stomach.

'Looking forward to it,' I lied.

I drove to the group session a few weeks later. But once I'd turned off the engine, I couldn't get out of the car. It felt like I'd been pressured to go on a blind date, but with four other people and a chaperone.

What if I have nothing in common with these people? What if I'm the only weirdo, and it's confirmed to me that all of my obsessions are actually true? Or what if they're all loopy? Would that make me loopy, too? These thoughts cycled through my head while I kept an eye on my watch. As much as I was dreading this experience, my stubborn need to be on time trumped my fear.

Two women were sitting on the chairs in the waiting room. One looked slightly older than me, the other slightly younger. Both seemed like normal, functioning members of society. I'm certain I could sense in them a feeling of relief that perhaps I looked like a 'respectable' person, too—whatever that means.

'Are you both here for the group session?' I asked.

The slightly younger one looked relieved that someone had broken the silence. 'Yep! Fuck, I'm so nervous,' she blurted out. 'Are you guys nervous?'

'Oh man, I didn't sleep last night. I'm shitting myself,' said the slightly older one.

I breathed an enormous sigh of relief. I could already tell that I would love these women.

Ten minutes later, there were five of us sitting in a semi-circle around Dr Wallace in a small room. I could sense a clear feeling of trepidation, but it felt different from the fear of my first psychologist session, perhaps because there was safety in numbers. Or maybe it was because we all felt a sense of solidarity, even though none of us had spoken yet.

Dr Wallace was beaming. She looked triumphant. She welcomed us and explained why she'd decided to bring us all together. She'd never convened an informal group before, but she was certain that we'd all gain so much from listening to each other. It wasn't difficult to share her optimism. It was clear that all of these people adored Dr Wallace as much as I did. I assumed that they'd all trusted her enough to guide them through terrifying and strange exposures, so why wouldn't we now trust her with this idea?

That first session was full of tears, laughter and head-nodding. Hearing other people talk about obsessions and compulsions that largely mirrored my own was a bizarre and liberating experience. I'd never spoken to anyone else who had OCD before. Not once in my 31 years. And suddenly I was surrounded by four wonderful souls who had experienced the same torment throughout most of their lives.

I wasn't the only one in the world who had called the AIDS hotline on more than 100 occasions, or pieced together the minute-by-minute events of a boozy night—with the same precision that a crime investigator would use to solve a cold-blooded murder—to convince myself that I hadn't cheated on my boyfriend. I wasn't the only one to worry that I was a paedophile or to check my son and daughter for signs of breathing multiple times before going to bed. I experienced a feeling of belonging and camaraderie that was almost overwhelming. It really is a magical thing to be freed from such crippling isolation, and I have no doubt that this freedom has been one of the most significant factors in my recovery from OCD.

THE BENEFITS OF GROUP THERAPY

Ever since starting group therapy, I've sung its praises from the rooftops. I'll bang on about it to anyone who'll listen. Having access to a group of people who have lived through similar experiences, and who just *get it*, has been life-changing.

According to the American Psychological Association, group therapy is as effective as individual therapy.[1] It's cost-effective to run, since facilitators can see more than one person at a time, and cheaper than one-on-one sessions. Unfortunately, group therapy hasn't quite taken off in Australia as much as it has in other countries. While it's very common to come across people who see a therapist in a one-on-one context, I barely know anyone who is part of a group for mental health support. Traditionally, not many places have offered group therapy, possibly because of the extra training required to facilitate groups effectively. Additionally, in the past, group sessions haven't been subsidised. Luckily, this is slowly changing.

Baring your innermost fears can be hard enough to do with one person, let alone a group of people you don't know. If you decide to start group therapy, then you'll likely feel raw and vulnerable at the beginning. But if you remind yourself that everyone else is feeling the same fears and fighting similar doubts, then it might make the prospect less daunting.

Below are a few reasons why group therapy is a powerful mental health tool.

THE POWER OF THE PEER

OCD can be an isolating illness. Because we often feel like we're 'bad' or 'weird' or even a danger to others, we can shut ourselves off, believing that we're the only ones in the world who feel this way. Meeting others who have shared experiences with OCD (and this doesn't have to mean the same OCD obsessions) can help us shed the shame that has enveloped us for so long. It also reminds us that OCD isn't our fault—it's separate from us.

Clinical psychologist Dr Claire Ahern, facilitator of OCD Online Programs at Melbourne Psychology & Counselling, has witnessed the power of peer support many times while running online group-therapy sessions.

'The obsessions really target whatever we care about. They want to hit you in the guts. Because of that, there's nothing so powerful as being around others and recognising that they're accepting you for who you are. It's powerful to get that from your therapist or professionals around you, but to get that from someone else who experiences OCD—and to be able to provide that to another person—is so connecting and rewarding,' she explains.

Dr Ahern is passionate about offering group-therapy options, and while she has noticed that it can take a while for people to take the plunge, she has seen numerous clients gain from it once they do.

'There's always this moment: we're talking, and then I step back and see that everyone else is talking and doing their thing. I just love that so much. I think there's something about getting people together and realising there's more in common than not. There's lots of shared humanness there. It's destigmatising,' she says.

TARGETING SHARED BELIEF SYSTEMS

Some people might feel hesitant to join group therapy for fear of having to talk about their particular obsessions. They might worry that no one else will relate to the same themes as them. However, one of the aims of group therapy is to target the belief systems that continue to fuel OCD.

'The content of the obsession doesn't matter. It's what it means to them that matters. I want to show people that there are similarities between them. Belief systems are similar, even if the symptom presentations are different,' explains Dr Ahern.

NEW TOOLS AND ACCOUNTABILITY

With multiple people comes multiple perspectives, and you'll probably find that you learn a lot from others who have OCD. It's likely that different group members will be at different stages in their treatment and recovery, so seeing the tools that others use to cope and thrive can be beneficial.

Being part of a group can also hold you accountable in ways that you may not experience with one-on-one therapy. Because exposure and response prevention (ERP) can be so uncomfortable, it's easy to drop it down the list of priorities and come up with a hundred reasons why it's just not the right time to do it. But seeing others diving into their treatment can be a great motivator.

SUPPORT NETWORK

After my first few group sessions, the other members and I decided to set up a WhatsApp group so that we could stay in touch between sessions. Often our messages won't have anything to do with OCD, but every now and then someone will discuss something difficult that they're going through or ask others for ERP advice. Because we've learned not to give each other (too much) reassurance, we instead help each other to sit with uncertainty and also provide understanding and empathy.

Different kinds of group therapy

Currently, there isn't a wide variety of options for group therapy in Australia, but with research increasingly demonstrating the benefits—both for the wider health system and individuals—this is starting to change.

Group therapy run by a clinician

These sessions will be run by a psychologist, with the aim of using psychoeducation and therapeutic approaches to change mindsets and/or behaviours. It's likely that the sessions will be structured.

Support groups

Some places offer support groups that are run by a facilitator, but they won't necessarily be a trained clinician. The aims of these groups are to provide support and a safe and confidential space for people to share their experiences, and to encourage members to learn from each other. Support groups are often free and are likely to be less formal than group therapy.

Telehealth

Group therapy doesn't have to be done in person. Since the Covid-19 pandemic, more places are offering telehealth for both individual and group sessions. Telehealth involves consulting with a mental health care professional by video call or phone. Most providers will prefer that you have access to video and will often use platforms such as Zoom or Skype, which require high speed internet access on a computer.

Various research carried out since the early 2000s has found that telehealth-based treatments are generally as effective for OCD as face-to-face treatments.[2]

A note on rebates

In Australia, people with OCD are now eligible for up to ten group-therapy sessions under their Mental Health Treatment Plan. These are separate from the allocated individual sessions. You don't have to be doing one-on-one treatment to start group therapy, and some clinics offer telehealth options for group therapy.

This kind of support is like suddenly being able to jump in an enclosed trampoline when before you were bouncing on one of those nineties net-free death traps, never knowing if you'd be launched off or snag a limb between the springs. You suddenly feel so safe and supported. I realise that not all groups will gel in this way, but even having access to a network during the therapy sessions can be life-changing.

RELAPSE

After seeing Dr Andrea Wallace for over a year, joining group therapy and doing regular exposures, I felt like I could see a 'way out' of OCD for the first time ever. I wasn't completely symptom-free, but I was no longer tortured by obsessions and compulsions all the time. In fact, there were days—even weeks—when I barely registered them. It was such a huge relief. I started to see my life unfold before me without the oppressive filter of OCD.

During a group session that was being run online thanks to the Delta Covid-19 strain, Dr Wallace asked us to check in with everyone and give our OCD a ranking from one to ten (one being barely present, and ten being always present). I gave mine a three. I said something along the lines of 'I feel like I'm in recovery. I barely get any obsessions these days, and I feel almost free of OCD. Although I'm probably going to jinx myself now . . . ha-ha.'

Dr Wallace would tell me there's no such thing as jinxing yourself, but two days later I fell into an OCD hole so deep and dark that it felt like I'd never resurface. I can see now that this was always going to happen at some stage, but at the time I cursed myself for being so outwardly cocky about feeling 'almost free of OCD'.

I had two kids under the age of three in one of the strictest and longest Covid-19 lockdowns in the world. My partner was still able to work, but I was stuck at home with a baby who screamed from the moment she came out of the womb until she was nine months old, and a restless toddler who tested my limits and made me question my parenting skills every minute of every day.

The washing pile was hitting the ceiling, the floors of our house were littered with toys and dog hair, and I was tormented by that tedious question of 'What the fuck am I going to cook for dinner?', only to then have that resentfully made dinner hurled onto the ground by my toddler. At some stage, something was bound to give.

In the past, I'd experienced OCD thoughts focused on paedophilia. For me (and for many others, I imagine), nothing is worse than the fear of being a paedophile. I love kids, and obviously I have my own kids. The thought of any child in distress makes me feel physically ill, which is why this theme lodged itself so insidiously into my head. I can't remember what triggered this particular episode, but somehow I'd convinced myself—within the space of a few hours—that I was a sadistic monster whom kids couldn't be safe around. I was starting to question everything, and I became so distressed that for a few days I could barely get myself out of bed. Depressive feelings mingled with panic. If I wasn't lying down or having a shower, trying to think my way out of my fear, I was trying to get reassurance from Hugh.

I'd never talked in great detail to Hugh about my obsessions, but on this occasion I told him about what was going through my head. He patiently listened to my distressed ramblings and offered the comfort I was so desperately seeking. But the solace was fleeting; within an hour, I was again under siege from my own mind, feeling fragile and afraid.

Luckily, within a few days I was able to make an appointment with Dr Wallace, and she deftly guided me out of my OCD hole once again. She reminded me of the importance of differentiating between thoughts and behaviours. Within a day or so, I was able to see the absurdity in my fear, but I was genuinely rattled by the speed and intensity with which this fear was able to take hold and pin me down.

It was a sunny yet crisp winter's day in Melbourne, and accountants all around the country were nursing hangovers from a big night on the town celebrating the end of the financial year. My third child, Patrick, had been born eighteen hours earlier, and I was feeling elated, delirious and sore. He had just slipped into a noisy sleep, and I was reclining the back of my hospital bed in the desperate hope that I could nod off for an hour or so. Suddenly the door swung open, and a young woman glided in with a huge trolley, explaining that she was going to test Patrick's hearing.

'Fuck off,' I said in my head.

'No worries,' I said out loud.

I'm eternally grateful that we have access to this kind of intervention in our hospitals, and there's no doubt that it improves outcomes for babies with hearing loss. I was just so painfully tired.

The audiologist skilfully fitted three electrode pads to him and started playing some gentle sounds to test his nerve and brain response. She kept rearranging the pads and frowning. Patrick was becoming irritable, and after about five minutes she took the pads off him and told me she wasn't getting a response.

'Not to worry,' she chirped. 'We can try again tomorrow. This happens quite frequently; he might be too unsettled.'

The next day, another audiologist turned up to conduct the test again. Once more, she couldn't get a response from Patrick. 'It doesn't mean he's deaf,' she told me, aware of the panic in my voice when I asked her if she could run the test again. 'He might have fluid in his ears. You can try again in a week or so.'

But that uncertainly was enough to send me over the edge. For the next week, I was convinced that my new baby was deaf. I googled the percentage of babies that fail the first few tests and called everyone I knew who had kids, asking if they, too, had experienced a number of tests before getting the all clear. But even once he did pass the test a week later, my mind turned to other possible health and neurological issues that he might be diagnosed with down the track.

I'm very aware that this kind of health anxiety is common for new parents, but I knew where this was heading. I could feel myself descending into a dangerous and familiar pit. I was struggling to feel any joy; all I felt were waves of panic whenever I looked at him. I was convinced that he would grow up to be diagnosed with some kind of neurological disorder . . . because I'd taken antidepressants throughout the pregnancy.

Luckily, I was able to have regular online sessions with Dr Wallace throughout this period, and she told me what I didn't want to hear: do more exposures. She helped me to come up with a bunch of exposures, and I'd have to do them throughout the week. Because I was seeking so much reassurance from my family, I had to tell them to stop reassuring me. I'd also find articles about early signs of various disorders to get my anxiety up, and then try to sit with the discomfort of not knowing.

I'd make loop tapes to articulate the fears, listening to myself say things like 'Maybe Patrick will be diagnosed with something down the track, and maybe he won't? Perhaps he will one day be diagnosed with a health condition so devastating it will change everything. But maybe he will be healthy. Maybe he won't hit any of his developmental milestones. But maybe he will hit them all. I don't know for sure. And I'm still safe in that not-knowing.'

After a few weeks of doing exposures, and once Patrick's sleep had improved, the OCD calmed down and the health fears dissipated.

MY TAKEAWAYS

I learned three valuable lessons from my relapses:

1. I may never be completely free of OCD. At first this realisation seemed depressing, but I don't see it that way anymore. I've taken the pressure off myself to beat it and now put my energies into understanding it.
2. I was never starting from scratch after each relapse. Having a relapse after a period without symptoms will feel scary, but it's important to remind yourself that you have access to tools to drag yourself out of the OCD hole. Every time you do this, you'll learn more.

3. If I pre-empt a relapse and put supports in place, I'll be better off. I knew when I was pregnant with my third child that my OCD would spike throughout the perinatal period, which prompted me to be more vigilant with seeing my psychologist, reaching out and doing exposures.

Try not to see a relapse as a failure. Look at it as a chance to learn more about your OCD so that you're better equipped to manage it next time a relapse happens.

LAPSE vs RELAPSE

In their book, *Everyday Mindfulness for OCD*, Jon Hershfield and Shala Nicely describe a lapse as a temporary OCD flare-up (perhaps you respond fearfully to a thought and do a compulsion or two) and a relapse as a more prolonged period when symptoms return to the intensity of your OCD at its worst. They point out that lapses, or slips, will often occur and are very normal. But it's when the slips become more frequent, intense and persist for longer that they're likely to turn into a relapse. They encourage you to mindfully monitor your slips so that you can pre-empt a relapse with the tools you've been using to manage your OCD.[3]

In retrospect, my relapses didn't come out of the blue. I was slipping up and doing compulsions without even realising it. You won't catch every lapse, especially if you've had OCD symptoms for years, and that's okay.

CAN YOU OVERCOME OCD?

Many people, including myself, spend decades following certain thought and behaviour patterns to try to survive with OCD. These behaviours become very much entrenched. When we're triggered by something, we'll go down the same road we always do and end up in the world of compulsions before we even know what we're doing.

When I ask clinical psychologist Dr Victoria Miller if it's possible to overcome OCD completely, she explains that while you can change your behavioural responses to triggering thoughts, you can't change the actual thoughts themselves.

'You can dial down the volume, you can accept their presence. But if you define having unwanted thoughts as a symptom of OCD, then you're never going to feel symptom-free. But hopefully you can get to a point where you can accept that that's not what OCD is—that having unwanted thoughts is the human experience. And the OCD part is the behaviour that comes in to manage the distress associated with that experience," Dr Miller says.

CHANGING THE NEURAL PATHWAYS

Without needing to ask everyone who has OCD, I can confidently say that no one likes doing exposures. It's a fact. If we liked doing them, then they wouldn't be exposures—and we wouldn't have OCD. When I first started therapy with Dr Andrea Wallace, I thought that I'd only have to do ERP for a short, intense period and then I'd triumphantly hang up my ERP boots. Dr Wallace would often talk about the importance of doing ERP therapy regularly, but I'd conveniently filter this to mean that *some people* need to do that. But *I'd* be fine without it.

Unfortunately, that's not the case. I've come to realise that I might always have to do some form of ERP. Not every day, not every week and not even every month. But I won't necessarily get to the point where I can be finished with it completely.

When I ask clinical psychologist Dr Celin Gelgec, Director of the Melbourne Wellbeing Group, about the importance of regular ERP therapy, she explains it in a really helpful way.

'The best recipe for encoding information [storing information in our long-term memory] is when we have a trigger that's linked to thoughts, that's then followed with a behaviour [obsession or compulsion]. When our amygdala—the emotion centre of our brain—is going off, the first thing it does is talk to our long-term memory system. It's like, "What works in this situation? Quick no time for logic, I need an answer!"

'And if you're doing that nearly all day, every day, for a long time, it's tattooed onto your brain. But when we do ERP, we have the trigger, we have the thoughts and feelings, but we *don't* have the behaviour that follows through. So, the reinforcer is diminished. And this is why consistency and repetition in our treatment is important. Because you need to do that often enough for the brain to even *register* a new option of responding, and for that new pathway to be established,' Dr Gelgec explains.

In summary, when this new pathway you create by doing ERP starts to override the OCD pathway, your symptoms will diminish. With persistence and maintenance, there's a very good chance that you can not only manage your symptoms but also become symptom-free—or at least as *close* to symptom-free as it's possible to be.

Chapter 11

THE FUNNY SIDE

It wasn't until I started group therapy—and talking more frequently about my obsessions and compulsions—that I began to occasionally laugh at my OCD. The more I externalised my OCD and shared my experiences, the more distant it seemed from me. It was like stepping away from my own shadow, a darkness I'd been afraid of for so long. When you can't see something properly, you're more likely to jump to fearful conclusions. But once light is shone onto it and the gaps are filled in, you're more likely to understand it and relate to it. Learning more about OCD through therapy, books and talking to others with OCD allowed me to look at it with more curiosity and incredulity than fear.

I'm not suggesting that all I do now is laugh in the face of OCD like a deranged superhero, but the more I've used humour in my treatment, the looser OCD's grip has felt. Using humour won't be right for everyone at every stage of their OCD journey, and I want to point out that I'm not laughing at other people with OCD. One of the reasons OCD is so misunderstood is because of the perception that it's not as serious as other mental illnesses. It's often trivialised by those who don't understand it, and I don't want to add to this dangerous mockery. But being able to see the lighter side of my own experience and the absurdity of some of my obsessions and compulsions has helped me enormously.

GIGGLE THERAPY

Below are a few reasons why humour might help you, and ways you can incorporate it into your treatment. When my anxiety is particularly bad, I often start to take shorter and quicker breaths, making my heartbeat accelerate and my whole body feel tense. One of the ways I try to combat this, especially if I'm in the car or going for a walk, is to listen to a funny podcast. I often find that laughing out loud is a great way to help me regulate my breathing.

LAUGHTER CAN FIGHT STRESS HORMONES

When we have an obsession that triggers a stress response, it's likely that hormones such as cortisol and adrenaline are released. When we laugh, our body releases endorphins that counteract the stress hormones. A good laugh can also stimulate the circulation and relax your muscles, reducing some of the physical symptoms associated with stress.

LAUGHTER CAN INTERRUPT THE FALSE ALARM

When we experience the fight, flight or freeze response to stress, an alarm goes off in our brain to tell us we're in danger. With OCD, that alarm goes off every time an obsession is experienced, and we're flooded with stress multiple times a day. Interrupting this process with laughter can send a signal to our brain that we're not in danger and, in turn, our body can begin to relax.

When you feel triggered by an obsession, instead of diving headfirst into a compulsion, try delaying the behaviour by watching or listening to something that usually makes you laugh. This might be extremely difficult to do at first, because your stress response is firing, and laughing will probably be the last thing you feel like doing. But even if it works one out of every ten times, it's still a win—and it might help you to create those new neural pathways needed to overcome OCD symptoms.

LAUGHTER CAN GIVE YOU BACK A SENSE OF POWER

It's easier to laugh at our OCD when we can separate it from ourselves. When we learn that OCD doesn't define us, and we can achieve some mastery over it, we gain a sense of power. Clinical psychologist Dr Victoria Miller believes that humour, when used in the appropriate context, can be very therapeutic for OCD sufferers.

'Humour can be really nice, because it can help you bring attention to the ridiculousness of the moment. And it can be a great relational component to treatment that parents can use with their kids, or with partners, if you use it carefully, so you're not being patronising. So, they don't feel mocked,' she explains.

When I'm talking about my OCD with someone else who has it, I often find myself detaching from it, and looking at it with some amusement. Because suddenly it's something that other people deal with, too—it's not innately *mine*.

THE SILVER LININGS

In their book *Everyday Mindfulness for OCD*, Jon Hershfield and Shala Nicely discuss the flipside of having OCD: being what they call a 'noticer', which I touched upon in Chapter 5. They say that noticers are often creative, funny and compassionate. 'Long term mastery over OCD,' they explain, 'is not the elimination of this special kind of mind. *It is learning to fall in love with it.*'[1]

I'm not trying to bombard you with little nuggets of toxic positivity; at the end of the day, living with OCD is fifty shades of fucked. It's exhausting and debilitating. If I ever meet the genie from *Aladdin*, my first wish will be to live a life free

Cognitive diffusion

Cognitive diffusion, from acceptance and commitment therapy (ACT), is a tool that helps us to detach from our obsessions so we can see them for what they are: passing thoughts, feelings or urges. Interrupting this fusion between ourselves and our thoughts can help us to observe them rather than engage with them. I once heard someone say that it's like you're reading a book, and the TV is on in another room. You can hear the sounds from the TV, but you aren't engaging with them. This is how you can deal with your thoughts. They're still there, but you relate to them differently.

There are a few ways to use cognitive diffusion when doing exposure and response prevention (ERP):

- Notice the thoughts. If you get a thought such as *What if I'm a murderer?*, say something to yourself such as 'I'm noticing that I'm having a thought about being a murderer, and this feels really distressing.' This can be a really helpful way to diffuse the fear. You can say this out loud or in your head.
- Sing the thoughts. Croon some of your looping thoughts to the tune of a song. This can be a good way to change your relationship to the thought, by taking it less seriously.
- Thank the thoughts. When you experience an obsession, saying things such as 'Thanks for that interesting feedback' can help to deprive it of any important meaning.

Some people find that giving their OCD a name can help them to separate it from themselves.

from OCD. But until that happens, I know that I have to put up with my infuriating brain. Luckily, over the years I've found a few silver linings to my experience.

YOU HAVE TOOLS TO COPE WITH EVERY PART OF LIFE

Fear of uncertainty isn't something that only people with OCD have to manage; it's universal. It's just that most people don't develop a behaviour pattern that reinforces the fear that comes along with uncertainty. Learning how to sit with the discomfort of 'not knowing' is likely to help you in every facet of your life. Additionally, the tools you learn to use for OCD—for example, ERP, mindfulness and ACT—will also help you to weather all sorts of storms that come your way in life.

YOU CAN HARNESS YOUR CREATIVITY FOR GOOD

Most people with OCD have overactive and vivid imaginations. Our brains are annoyingly creative, which is why we can think of a thousand different ways that something could possibly go wrong before we've even opened our eyes in the morning. However, once you learn to manage your OCD and become better at staying in the moment, you'll be able to use your creative brain to bring yourself joy rather than misery.

YOU'RE NOT ALONE

I can guarantee that you're not alone in your despair: there are millions of people all around the globe who have OCD. While each person will experience it differently, the thread that connects us all is relying on a behaviour pattern to deal with our unwanted thoughts. It's likely that you already know a handful of people with OCD, but you may not realise it—it's very common for people to keep their diagnosis to themselves and conceal any obvious compulsions. But remember, vulnerability fuels connection. If you get to the point where you feel comfortable about sharing your experience, it may just encourage someone else to do the same.

Rick's story

'Hey, did I tell you about when I got locked out of the house stark naked last year?'

'Nope, but I can't wait to hear about it,' I reply. 'OCD?'

'Of course!'

Rick Davies looks a lot younger than his 40 years. A beloved Australian actor who shot to fame in 2010 playing the popular character of Jimmy in the TV show *Offspring*, he looks barely 30, with pale blue eyes and unruly blonde hair.

We've decided to meet at his local cafe in Thornbury. Within minutes of sitting down, he's almost knocked two oat lattes out of the waiter's hand while wildly gesticulating as he tells me about the latest humiliation he's had to suffer in the name of OCD.

One of Rick's obsessions started when he found a small trace of asbestos in his backyard a couple of years ago. It sent him into an absolute spin, but after a while the obsession subsided. Then, as he was preparing to build an outdoor shower in his backyard, he came across some old bricks covered in peeling paint. He wondered if it could be lead paint. He has a two-year-old son, so his mind started flipping through vague vignettes of information he'd read about lead exposure and how dangerous it can be for young children. Suddenly, he urgently needed an answer.

'I got some tested, and I thought it was all cool. But then the guy came back in and said, "Yeah, it is lead." And I just went, "Oh, fuck," and I felt myself begin to have a physiological response. I broke out in a sweat, knowing what my OCD was going to do with this. I was thinking, *This is going to exhaust my partner. This is going to exhaust me.* And then we are going to have an argument

down the track where I'm going to go, "At least you can walk away!"'
says Rick.

He tried not to let it overcome him, and a few days later he
continued with the digging to install the shower. But before he left
the backyard and entered the house, he'd have to go through a
lengthy decontamination process using the garden hose to ensure
that he didn't bring in any trace of lead that his son could ingest.

At the end of one particular day, he had already chucked out his
T-shirt, fearing it was contaminated. But before he could go inside,
his elderly Greek neighbour asked if Rick could help him move some
old timber in his backyard. Rick was sure that the timber also had
lead paint on it, so when he was finished—and before going back
inside his house—he also took off his shorts and undies, just in case.
After he'd once again washed himself thoroughly using the hose,
he turned the door handle to find that it was locked. His partner,
Channelle, was nowhere to be seen.

'Weirdly enough, I was just like, *I'm exhausted, and this feels
quite nice just standing here, nude,*' Rick recalls. 'But then I sensed
movement in the apartment block behind us. I'd been standing there
for twenty minutes at this stage. And then I saw this lady up there,
so I hid down behind the table and I was like, *She's seen everything
already,*' Rick says, cringing at the memory.

'Eventually, she opened the window and called out, "Are you
okay?" And I said, "I'm so sorry. I'm not a creep in somebody's backyard; I live here. My partner's locked me out. I'm so sorry you've
been subjected to this." Finally, Channelle came downstairs. I'm just
standing there naked and looking exhausted. She took one look at
me, and we both just pissed ourselves laughing.'

Spin doctor

Sometimes, when talking to Rick, it's hard to know if he's adding information to a story or trying to get reassurance about something that's worrying him. When I ask him about this, he says that Channelle often warns him about casually dropping references to asbestos and lead into conversations with people just in case he triggers someone else's OCD. But sometimes his compulsion will be more about letting other people know about possible dangers they could avoid.

'I guess it's part of my therapy to actually sit on that sort of stuff, which feels unbelievably irresponsible when it's really bad and you feel like you're killing everybody,' Rick says with a pained smile.

The backyard nudity incident wasn't the first time that OCD had put Rick in a humiliating position, but he's always able to deftly spin an embarrassing experience into a hilarious anecdote.

I ask him if OCD has helped or hindered him in his career as an actor and writer, Is he creative because of, or in spite of, his OCD?

'With some of the situations that you find yourself in, you just go, *Fuck, how am I going to get out of this? What am I going to do to make this person think that everything is totally normal and there's nothing to see here?* By the very nature of OCD and the situations you find yourself in, you have to be creative. To find some sort of equilibrium again, just to function in society,' Rick says.

Rick articulates this perfectly. The extra work that people with OCD have to do to try to conceal compulsions—to avoid any extra shame—can feel like a really shitty full-time job.

While he often struggles to stay present due to the thoughts cycling through his mind, acting has always been something he can do to escape OCD.

'I find acting and writing to be a real oasis, an escape, if I really commit. You give yourself permission in a way to jump out of OCD for a while.'

Growing up with OCD

Rick was eighteen when he was diagnosed with OCD, but he's had symptoms since he can remember. He remembers obsessively washing his hands when he was barely preschool age, and as he got older the obsessions morphed and intensified. Attending a school in Melbourne with compulsory religious classes, he started to develop a prayer compulsion whenever an intrusive thought entered his head. At first the compulsion was discreet, but over time it became more obvious to others.

One weekend, when he was at the beach with some mates, he was besieged by an unwanted thought. Without knowing what he was doing, he tightly shut his eyes, stuck his fingers in his ears and started to mutter the prayer he used to counteract the thought. When he was done, he opened his eyes to find that he'd wandered 100 metres down the beach, with all of his friends staring at him with unbridled bewilderment.

Not long after, while studying for his Year 12 exams, it all became too much. He was so overwhelmed by the noise in his head that he punched a wall. His mum sprang into action, making an appointment for him with a psychiatrist, who diagnosed him with OCD and started him on medication.

'When I say that I punched the wall, I like to think I did a big Hulk-hit through the wall, my hand coming out the other side of the house—but it was just the slightest knuckle hole in there. But

I was a very exhausted eighteen-year-old, studying for his Year 12 exams,' says Rick.

He doesn't so much talk as perform. If you didn't recognise him from TV, it would still be obvious that Rick's in the entertainment business. I love talking to him about OCD, because we always end up laughing about it. It's like talking about a mutual friend who always gets drunk and does weird shit. It becomes separate from us, and the shame we've internalised softens for a while.

When I ask him if humour has helped him deal with OCD throughout his life, he says that his family members—while always being his biggest supporters—have brought a lightness to his diagnosis. This has, in turn, helped him to deal with it all.

'I'd always ask for reassurance from my dad about things. Once I asked him something, I can't remember what it was about, and he said, "Yeah mate, no worries. I mean your dick will drop off, but that's fine." And then the joke kept on evolving. I'd ask a question, and Dad would just go, "Clunk." And then he'd look down around my feet. Mum thought it was hilarious, and I'd laugh as well.'

Humour won't help everyone, in every situation—and obviously it must be used with care and respect for the person with OCD—but I can tell that for Rick, it's been vital to his recovery.

'OCD has robbed me of a lot of present moments. But it's also fucking funny. I think the more you get to know your demons, the more you can shine a light on them. The shadows become a lot smaller, but it doesn't mean they go away. And if I'm not careful, the shadows can grow very long very quickly,' he explains.

Rick's been seeing a therapist for years, and has been on and off medication. I ask him if he's at peace with his OCD, but then immediately withdraw the question, because mentioning 'peace' and

'OCD' in the same breath seems laughable. But if anyone is going to humour me and answer my question, it's Rick.

'At times I really am, and at times I just hate it. I acknowledge how privileged I am, how lucky I am to have the support I do, but I still find it incredibly hard. But then, there are times when I'm working and the figurative sun is shining, and I'm like, *How good is all of this?*'

Rick is currently writing the script for a TV series about OCD, which he's found to be both infuriating and therapeutic. He's hopeful that by mining some of his painful experiences and then crafting them into something both honest and funny, he can help to tackle the misconceptions around OCD and put a positive spin on the anguish he's experienced.

'Now that I'm working on a show that we hope will get up, it's like, *Right, let's dive deep into it and get OCD to start pulling its weight.*'

Chapter 12

KIDS AND OCD

'How do I know if my kid has OCD?' This is a question I hear a lot. Sometimes kids carry out obvious compulsions, but for others, especially if they're still very young, it can be a difficult illness to diagnose. Many children are also embarrassed by their symptoms and try hard to hide them, which can add another layer of difficulty to the process.

Clinical psychologist Dr Rebecca Anderson, Director of the Curtin Psychology Clinic in Perth, explains that obsessive behaviour can be a normal developmental stage for some kids.

'It can be tricky, especially with the young ones. Around the age of five, it can be normal for your kid to arrange all their cars in a row, or to organise their books perfectly once they've learned what a spine is on a book. And that can go with a bit of angst. You're trying to get out the door, and they just can't disengage from that [activity], because they feel like they've got to finish it before they can leave. So, some of that is completely normal,' she explains.

She advises parents to ask themselves the following questions to try to tease out whether the behaviour their child is displaying falls into this 'normal' category or if it might be an indication of something deeper going on:

- Is this behaviour ongoing? Has this been going on for more than a couple of months?
- Has it worsened over time?
- Is it so rigid that it's starting to have an impact on the family?
- How is the behaviour impacting their functioning?
- Are there other times when they're able to be flexible with it?
- How distressed is the young person if they can't engage in the compulsions that they're trying to engage in?

In a nutshell, if the behaviour is ongoing, the child is distressed when they can't engage in their compulsions, and it's starting to have an impact on the functioning of the family, then it would be a wise idea to seek help from a child psychologist.

Psychiatrist Dr Chris Wever, who has 30 years of experience working with children, adolescents and families, agrees with Dr Anderson.

'The two words here are distress and disability. They're the two cornerstones for any diagnosis. If someone is not distressed and it doesn't cause any disability, it's not so much a disorder.

But if it causes distress and disability for them or their loved ones, then it's a problem,' he explains.

However, not all kids with OCD will carry out obvious compulsions, so Dr Anderson suggests that as parents we start to ask direct questions about our child's worries in a particular situation.

'Do they have any scary thoughts of the house burning down and everyone dying? And you can ask those direct questions. I don't think there's a too-young age that you can ask those questions to try to find out what it is that they're worrying about. If they're worrying about monsters in the bedroom at night, you can ask those questions and see if they've got any awareness of those cognitions.

'Asking about it doesn't bring on thoughts about death and dying; the kids are having them anyway. And the problem is that OCD can manifest in so many ways. I've had kids in my clinic who've had distressing intrusive thoughts like: *What if I stab Mum with a knife?* So, we've got to be able to ask these questions, even in those really little kids,' she says.

Dr Wever, who has written a book aimed at kids with OCD called *The Secret Problem,* says that sometimes parents need to be tactical in the way they seek out the information.

'No one's going to tell you that they have paedophilic thoughts or something, you know? That's secret. They don't want to tell anyone. So, there are certain ways of questioning kids to make them feel comfortable, like "Some kids have . . .", and then you go through a whole lot of weird thoughts, and make it very neutral, and then they go, "Oh, I've got that."'

Common symptoms in child and adolescent OCD

Obsessions	Compulsions
Contamination fears	**Cleansing rituals**
• germs	• hand-washing
• body fluids	• avoidance of contaminated
• environmental toxins, chemicals	substance
	• order or routine in washing
Intrusive, unpleasant thoughts or images	**Checking, repeating or avoidance rituals**
• harm or disaster befalling them	• checking doors, power points
• fear they will obey an OCD impulse	or themselves for self-injury or illness
• belief they're immoral, offending God or sexually deviant because of their OCD thoughts	• repeating behaviours
	• avoidance of triggers for obsessions
	• confessing or seeking reassurance that they're not bad people
Symmetry and order	**Ordering or balancing rituals**
• need for things to be symmetrical or balanced	• arranging things in order or straightening or lining up
• need for things to feel 'just right'	• counting or doing things a certain number of times
	• touching things with both sides of the body
Hoarding or collecting	**Hoarding**
• fear they will need things in the future	• collecting rituals in public
• objects have feelings and can't be discarded	• bedroom filled with non-useful items or multiples of one object
• a feeling that things can't be thrown away	

Source: Adapted from C. Wever, 'Obsessive-compulsive disorder in children and adolescents', *Australian Doctor*, September 2015. Used with permission of Australian Doctor Group.

FINDING HELP

Taking the first steps to find professional help for your child can be daunting, but if things are difficult and your child is regularly distressed, it's the right thing to do. Speaking with a professional will also take the pressure off you as a parent or carer. Treating OCD can often feel counterintuitive, especially if you have been giving your child regular reassurance or accommodating their compulsions. Additionally, the treatment will often need to include the support and understanding of the whole family, so getting guidance will make your lives easier in the long run.

THE ROLE OF A GOOD GP

Getting a diagnosis is obviously an important first step towards treating OCD. However, it's also extremely beneficial to talk to a GP that you trust and who understands OCD and how it's treated. Having a doctor on side who can point you in the right direction for further help will be crucial in this journey. For tips on how to find the right GP, turn to Chapter 4.

ONLINE, SELF-DIRECTED TREATMENT

I know from experience that finding help for your child is *way* easier said than done. It appears that all mental health professionals are currently working at absolute capacity, but the paediatric system seems to be the most clogged up. People are on waiting lists for months, even *years*, to see some specialists. This can turn an already stressful situation into an unbearable one.

At the end of this book, you'll find a useful Resources list. One of those resources is an online program called *OCD? Not Me!* that was created by Dr Rebecca Anderson and her team at Curtin University. This eight-stage, fully automated and anonymous program is designed for twelve- to eighteen-year-olds, and it can be done with or without the assistance of a therapist. Dr Anderson developed this online, gold-standard program because she saw a gap in treatment options for young people who were struggling but didn't necessarily require face-to-face help.

'For many people, these low-intensity online programs are enough. And then you can reserve things like your group therapies, your individual therapies and your inpatient stays for the pointier-end clients who have more complexity, where there's more risk involved. And they're your more expensive treatments as well. So, that's a really good way to spend money in the health system—to offer online programs at that low-intensity level,' explains Dr Anderson.

Another important reason for the creation of the online program was to help standardise treatment for OCD.

'We know that a lot of clinicians don't do exposure and response prevention [ERP] therapy well, and it's a big problem. If you google "OCD therapist", you'll get hundreds of names come up, but not all of them do ERP in the way it's meant to be done. So, this was a way of standardising some of the therapy, so that young people would be getting the structured ERP that we know is effective for OCD,' continues Dr Anderson.

Another great online option for both kids with OCD and their parents is Natasha Daniels' YouTube page and website (www.anxioustoddlers.com). A child anxiety and OCD therapist based in the United States, Natasha also has three kids with anxiety and OCD. She knows her topic *very* well. Her YouTube channel houses hundreds of helpful videos that are relatable and straightforward. She also offers courses for parents to help their kids with OCD, and ones specifically for kids and teens. There's also a parent community group you can join if you want access to support and information from other parents who are on the OCD roller-coaster with their kids.

These options are great if you're currently finding it difficult to locate a therapist, if your child is refusing to see a therapist or if the cost of seeking regular help is too high.

FACE-TO-FACE TREATMENT

If you think your child needs face-to-face treatment, then clinical psychologist Cassie Lavell, co-director at the Centre for Anxiety & OCD (CAO) on the Gold Coast, has some advice about what to look for when researching therapists. When searching for therapists online, ask yourself the following questions:

- Is their treatment approach to OCD clear?
- Do they mention cognitive behavioural therapy (CBT)?
- More importantly, do they offer ERP? If there's no information about that on their website, but they do treat OCD, give them a call and ask.

Once you've found a therapist that offers ERP, email or call them and ask the following questions:

- How much experience do they have in using ERP?
- Do they involve family in therapy? (This is preferable.)
- Do they perform the ERP *during* the session? (This is preferable.)

'You essentially want to interview your potential therapist, which I think is totally fair enough, because you need to make sure that they're the right fit for the child. It's expensive and waiting lists are long. You don't want to be on the waiting list for months to see someone, only to find out that they've never heard of ERP,' explains Lavell.

HOW TO TREAT KIDS DIAGNOSED WITH OCD

For mild cases of OCD, treating kids using ERP can be very effective. For more severe cases, a combination of ERP and medication is often used.

EXPOSURE AND RESPONSE PREVENTION (ERP)

Just like with adults, using a specific form of CBT called exposure and response prevention (ERP) is very effective for treating kids diagnosed with OCD. It's important that a licensed mental health professional (a psychologist, psychiatrist or counsellor) guides the child through the therapy. To read more about ERP, turn to Chapter 8.

Since ERP can be daunting, it should be introduced to kids gently and gradually. The therapist will start by discussing with the child the language around the obsessions and compulsions, and the anxiety that the obsessions provoke.

The specific strategies used will depend on the age of the child, but Dr Chris Wever starts with a ranking system.

'We develop a hierarchy of things, from the easiest to the hardest, and then we say, "Okay, we're going to start to use some exposure for the things that are lower on your list." We do that and then we sit with the anxiety until it dissipates. That's a learning experience for them: that anxiety will go away even if they don't do the OCD ritual. And then you give them a bit of homework. It doesn't matter if they can't do it. It's just playing with the OCD, not getting too serious about it, and just saying, "What can you do?,"' he explains.

Cassie Lavell says that to treat really young kids using ERP, she has to get a bit creative.

'You can do it with a five-year-old, but it's behavioural, really rewards-driven, and uses simple language about being brave. For example, I might say, "So your anxiety wants you to do this. Can we try to be brave and fight the anxiety?" And once they have completed the exposure task, we can reward them for doing something that's hard for them,' she explains.

FAMILY INVOLVEMENT

One of the most difficult things about OCD is that performing compulsions only alleviates anxiety temporarily—in the long term, it actually fuels the devastating obsessive–compulsive cycle. And when your child has OCD, it's easy to start accommodating their compulsions. You don't want to see your child in distress, so *understandably* you want to reassure them or give in to their compulsions if it seems to minimise their discomfort. Parents or carers doing this will always have loving intentions, BUT we know that this only makes the OCD *stronger*.

Kids never live in a bubble—they're part of a complex and interwoven family or community network, which is why it's so important to include those closest to them in their therapy. Once you understand how the accommodation is fuelling the OCD rather than helping it, it becomes easier to stop. Parents and carers can learn to become substitute ERP therapists at home, coaching kids to resist their compulsions. However, since kids are often used to their parents accommodating their compulsions, this resistance is usually introduced slowly.

'Doing it gradually helps the parent and the child,' suggests Cassie Lavell, who works with kids of all ages with anxiety and OCD. 'Start with a small step. For example, lots of kids with OCD have night-time rituals where there might be certain rules that the parent has to follow for bedtime to go smoothly. They might have to say "I love you" three times. They might have to kiss them on the forehead three times, and they might have to walk out of the room at a certain time. So that parent might pick one part of that ritual to stop first as opposed to just removing the whole ritual.'

Dr Chris Wever gives parents specific language and phrases to practise that will help their kids to resist compulsions at home.

'If your kid says to you, "Oh, please, please just reassure me one more time that I haven't done anything bad," you need to say, "Well, Dr Wever told me to say that it's your OCD, and that I need to try not to reassure you." And if it's too distressing, then you may say, "Okay, the OCD's too strong at the moment. Yep, we will reassure you this time, but we're going to have to work on that a little bit the next time." So, it's not torturing the kid. It's a matter of just building up their resilience slowly,' he explains.

It's also helpful to share the diagnosis with other important and trusted people in the child's life, such as their teacher, their grandparents and even some of their friends, so that no one is unintentionally fuelling the OCD outside of the home. However, you need to be sure that the person understands the OCD cycle and helps rather than hinders the therapy.

COMBINING CBT AND MEDICATION

According to Dr John S. March, if a child or adolescent is started on a small dose of medication, which is increased gradually, and this is done alongside CBT, then this will result in them getting the *best* results with the *least* amount of side effects and staying on the *lowest* possible dose.[1]

Some kids won't need medication; in mild to moderate cases of OCD, it's recommended that CBT is started with kids before medication is considered.

Medication

A landmark study published in the *Journal of the American Medical Association* found that there are clear benefits for children with OCD to use either CBT alone, or in combination with medication.[2] It's important to note that medication will not 'cure' OCD, but it's likely that symptoms will decrease significantly. Dr John S. March, Professor of Psychiatry and Behavioral Sciences at Duke University and author of *Talking Back to OCD*, says that choices made about what medication to start your child on should be based on patient preference, personal and family medical history, and expected side effects.[3]

SSRIs

If a child is experiencing severe OCD symptoms, or if they're too young to effectively benefit from CBT, a doctor may suggest starting them on medication. A selective serotonin reuptake inhibitor (SSRI) is the preferred form of medication, and currently two SSRIs are TGA-approved for kids with OCD:

- sertraline (Zoloft®)
- fluvoxamine (Luvox®)—for children from eight years of age.

Clomipramine (Anafranil®), a tricyclic antidepressant, used to be the medication of choice for OCD for many years. However, since SSRIs generally have fewer side effects, it's no longer the preferred medication for kids with OCD.

However, if a child has had two failed SSRI trials, this is when the doctor may look at clomipramine (Anafranil®) as an alternative (for children from ten years of age).[4]

Factors such as age, other medications and other medical conditions also need to be considered when deciding what medication to start your child on. Doctors can prescribe other medications if necessary.

Side effects

While it can be a scary concept to start any child on medication (especially when you read the warnings supplied), fewer than 5 per cent of children placed on an SSRI will need to discontinue it because of negative side effects.[5] However, almost all medications come with the potential for side effects, and these need to be weighed against the potential benefits of the drug. Some general side effects for SSRI medications include:[6]

- nausea
- agitation or nervousness
- sleepiness or insomnia.

Some children become more activated on SSRIs, so symptoms such as agitation, restlessness and disinhibition are more noticeable. A smaller number may become manic, in which case they would most likely need to stop the medication.[7]

The side effects of clomipramine (Anafranil®) can include dry mouth, weight gain and sedation, among others. It's important to discuss these with a medical professional.

Timing

Kids need to be started on medications slowly, with the dosage gradually increasing. Many kids won't respond for eight to twelve weeks, so a doctor will usually wait at least eight weeks before making any changes (unless the child is having negative reactions to the medication).

It's VERY important to note that any decision to stop a medication, start a new one or alter the dosage should always be made in consultation with your doctor.

HOW YOUNG IS TOO YOUNG FOR MEDICATION?

Dr Wever doesn't necessarily have an age limit for treating kids with medication for OCD. He says that the symptoms need to be assessed, and sometimes it's appropriate to start very young kids on very small doses of medication and monitor them carefully. There's currently no evidence to suggest that the medications used to treat OCD have any long-term side effects.

WILL MY CHILD NEED TO BE ON MEDICATION FOREVER?

According to Dr Chris Wever, once a child or adolescent has found a medication that works, they will generally need to stay on it for twelve to eighteen months. His reasoning? There are risks with coming off a medication too soon, but very little risk in staying on one for too long. His advice to parents is that if a child wants to come off their medication, this will need to be done over a period of around three to six months, tapering off very gradually. And the child will then need to be monitored to see whether the OCD comes back. If it does, the parent should get back in contact with the doctor.

It can be a difficult pill to swallow (pardon the pun), but some people will need medication throughout their lives to keep their OCD symptoms under control. There's absolutely nothing to be ashamed of if your child needs to keep taking medication to stay well. This can be a tough realisation to arrive at, and many people may want to set their child the goal of getting off medication. There's nothing wrong with that approach, but you must weigh up the costs and benefits of doing so. The aim is to live a full and rewarding life with minimal OCD symptoms.

WHAT IF NOTHING IS WORKING?

In some cases, if using one medication and CBT isn't working, then combining more than one medication may be an option. If nothing seems to be working, the child might need more specialised and intensive treatment at a clinic or hospital.

If you suspect your child has OCD, or if they have been diagnosed with OCD, please know that you can still live a fulfilling and happy life with the disorder. OCD doesn't have to define anyone, and it also doesn't have to be a barrier to hold them back from the life they want to live.

You will be left exasperated by their behaviour at times, but please remember that they are just as infuriated by themselves— the difference is that they can't escape their own mind.

Rose's story

OCD can be torturous for those experiencing it. But parenting a child with OCD can be just as agonising. Rose is still trying to process how her daughter went from being a carefree little girl to a teenager who was too afraid to open her eyes for fear that something bad would happen to anyone she looked at.

A flight attendant for the last 30 years, Rose has kind eyes and a warm demeanour. She's that attendant who smiles at you when you step onto the plane and makes you feel immediately at ease, allowing you to momentarily forget your crushing anxieties about the plane hurtling back down to earth (just me?).

In retrospect, Rose sees that her youngest child, Eadie, would occasionally display subtle but obsessive behaviours when she was in primary school, such as trying to take the 'correct' number of steps to get to the car, or needing to finish on the same spot on the netball court every time she practised her shots. But the behaviours didn't appear to be having an impact on her life—she was a sporty, social and smart young girl, and the behaviours looked like innocuous quirks to Rose at the time. Then, for a few years, it seemed like those behaviours had disappeared, so Rose was able to happily tuck away her parental concerns.

It wasn't until Rose and her husband separated, when Eadie was in Year 10, that things started to derail. Upon reflection, Rose believes that the uncertainty of this time caused her daughter to catastrophise and imagine the worst-possible scenario for every situation. Once a student who loved going to school, Eadie rapidly reached the point where she couldn't get out of the car once she and Rose had pulled up at the school gates.

'She couldn't articulate what was going on at the time, but I remember she went two days without sleeping or eating. She was just performing compulsions all day long. She would run out to the backyard and stick her head in the pool and pray. We actually had to lock her in the house, because she would also run out to the street and get down and kiss the road, regardless of anything that was coming or anybody who saw her. She got to the point where she couldn't hide. She was just punishing herself,' Rose recalls.

At the time, Rose didn't know what was driving these compulsions, but she later learned from Eadie that she was experiencing intrusive thoughts about being racist, which caused her to physically punish herself. She also felt that she'd be responsible for awful things happening to other people, unless she performed certain—often dangerous—rituals. This is often referred to as Magical Thinking OCD—where there's no logical connection between the fear and the compulsion.

Eadie was messy, disorganised and terrible at being on time. Rose had no idea that these were obsessive-compulsive behaviours, because—like so many others—she connected OCD with traits such as cleanliness and fastidiousness. But it was clear that her daughter's mental state was deteriorating at an alarming rate, and Rose was at a complete loss for how to help.

Hospitalisation

Initially, the school counsellor encouraged Eadie to write a diary to help her to express what was going on inside her head. But the situation only worsened, and soon Eadie couldn't hide her compulsions at school.

'The school counsellor rang me and said, "Okay, I'm seeing now. She can't hide it from me, and I'm seeing what you're seeing. We need to do something."'

However, Eadie's decline coincided with the unwelcome arrival of Covid-19 to Australian shores. The state government of Victoria announced tough Stage 3 restrictions to 'stop the spread', which made access to mental health treatment even more difficult than it usually is.

'We took her to emergency and had to go through police and temperature checks to even get into the hospital, because of the Covid-19 thing. Anyway, a doctor came in and talked to her, and at that point she's kissing the floor constantly, which was a compulsion. The doctors are panicking, putting masks on her and everything, and she just kept pulling them off. Anyway, then they said to me, "We are going to give her a bit of medication and send you home." And I just said, "No. I'm not going home."'

Normally someone to avoid conflict at any cost, Rose was instinctively discovering an assertive maternal strength. The desperate but unyielding lioness would protect her vulnerable cub at any cost.

They eventually conceded that she could remain in the short-stay area for two hours, which Rose felt was a minor victory.

'And then after a while, she just let loose. She started to get up on the bed and touch the roof and get back down again, get up on the bed, touch the roof and get on the floor, kiss the floor, over and over. And the nurses then started going, "Oh, okay, now we see what you're talking about."'

The decision was made to admit Eadie into the adolescent inpatient mental health unit at Monash Children's Hospital.

'We took her over to the ward, and I was distraught because I didn't realise I'd have to leave her there. I couldn't stay. But I was so desperate at that point,' says Rose, looking weary from the memory.

This was one of those decisions that most parents are lucky enough not to ever confront. Do I keep my child with me, even though they're experiencing an enormous amount of distress and pain, or do I leave them in an unfamiliar environment, put all my trust in the medical system and hope that my child improves (and forgives me for making this decision)? I can't help but think of my own little girl, currently three years old, and how hard it is on some days just to leave her at child care for six hours, when she's clinging to me with her tiny fingers and pleading with me to take her home. I try to imagine myself in Rose's shoes, leaving her daughter at a mental health ward as a teenager, and I start to feel an unwelcome lump in my throat.

Rose didn't sleep that night, thinking about her little girl alone in that small, sparse room. But she didn't know how much worse things were about to get.

'At six in the morning, I thought, *I'm going to ring and see how she is*. I rang and said, "I'm going to come in." And they're like, "No, we've shut the hospital down. You can come in at six o'clock tonight. It's one parent for fifteen minutes, and you have to be 2 metres away from her,"' Rose recalls, her eyes suddenly sparkling with tears that threaten to run down her face.

Lockdown laws had suddenly tightened, and Stage 4 restrictions were now in place. The blow that this news delivered to Rose still seems to be reverberating; the trauma is still raw and painful.

When Rose went in to visit Eadie, while maintaining a 2-metre distance, she noticed some blood on Rose's legs, and then throughout her sheets.

'On her bed there was a wooden base that stuck out from below the mattress. Once I noticed the blood, I found out that she had tucked her feet up behind her and slid off the bed. She'd damaged her legs so badly: she'd scraped all the skin off them, and her knees were inflamed. She ended up with sepsis from it. And no one had noticed,' says Rose, shaking her head incredulously.

After that, they had to move Eadie to the High Dependency Unit (HDU). They removed the base of the bed, so Eadie's mattress was on the ground.

'There were only five kids in the HDU. She stayed there for months, and there was no outdoor area. Going in there every day for six months ... it was really confronting and hard. Every night I would cry myself to sleep. But one thing I was so grateful for was that she always had a nurse with her,' says Rose.

For weeks, Rose could only visit Eadie for fifteen minutes a day, maintaining a 'safe' distance. It was torture for Rose, who wanted nothing more than to envelop her daughter in a warm and protective hug whenever she saw how distressed she was.

Finally, a diagnosis

With most airline staff grounded, Rose couldn't work throughout the lockdowns, so she started researching what could be driving her daughter to punish herself in such distressing ways. She was soon convinced it was OCD. After a few weeks, the doctors agreed with Rose and told her that Eadie had OCD, as well as clinical depression. Eadie was given diazepam (Valium®) every day just to calm the compulsions down, and to quieten the barrage of thoughts torturing her mind, as well as a selective seratonin reuptake inhibitor (SSRI), antipsychotics and lithium, for her depression.

But she would continue to find ways to punish herself when the thoughts became unbearable. Rose would often notice that when it looked like Eadie was sleeping, she was, in fact, holding her head up a few centimetres from the mattress—just enough so that she couldn't be comfortable, but not so much that the nurses would notice. Or she wouldn't let herself go to the toilet. Her bladder would be almost bursting (which a doctor noticed when she needed to have an MRI), but she wouldn't let herself feel the comfort and release until she just couldn't hold on anymore.

I notice that Rose talks about much of Eadie's time in hospital with a degree of detachment—almost as if she's telling someone else's story. I imagine that this is a defence mechanism, as she's still trying to recover from the waves of pain, fear and anxiety that were ceaselessly crashing against her during this period.

After six months, while Rose was packing up the family home, having just sold it, she received a call from the hospital.

'Three days before I was due to move, they called me in and said, "We really think it's important for her to see the house one last time, but we can't let her out for the day because of Covid-19. We have to completely discharge her, or she stays—there's no in between. But we really feel like it's important, and we just don't know what else to try." And I'm like, "Okay, well I'm packing up a house in three days to move, but I would do anything to get her home."'

By this point, Eadie was on a steady combination of medications, and was doing ERP treatment with a psychologist. However, she was still very unwell, and the compulsions continued to wreak havoc on her day-to-day life. But, to Rose's relief, Eadie gradually started to show signs of improvement.

'She just slowly started to relax. When she started doing compulsions such as wearing all her clothes backwards, I would suggest something like, "Why don't we pop that top on the right way for half an hour and then, if you feel uncomfortable, we'll swap it back? But let's just try." Over time she would try, and after about eight months she was able to wear her clothes the right way again,' says Rose.

Eadie had been discharged from hospital and was an outpatient with the Child and Youth Mental Health Service (CYMHS). She had a dedicated team of four people looking after her, and a psychologist would visit the house regularly for Eadie's appointments. Gradually, Eadie and Rose started to gain a better understanding of OCD, and Eadie was encouraged to look at her OCD as separate from herself.

'So, we called her OCD Tony, as she wanted a non-binary name for it. That was a game-changer for her. I would notice that she'd be quite distracted and I'd see the compulsion start to ramp up, and I'd be like, "Is Tony in your head again?" And she'd go, "Yeah." I'd go, "Well fuck Tony, I want some time with you."'

By this stage, Eadie had missed an entire school year, and it was time for Year 11 orientation. Luckily, the school was very accommodating and allowed Eadie to start back on her own terms; they agreed that she could get up and leave the classroom whenever necessary. Slowly, Eadie started to feel strong enough to attend school regularly. She graduated Year 12 at the end of 2022, and was accepted into a nursing course.

'I say to her, "You've learned more in your lifetime than most kids your age. It was an awful way to learn it, but it will make you an amazing nurse if that's what you choose to do,"' says Rose.

Once Eadie started doing acceptance and commitment therapy (ACT) alongside the ERP, she was better able to grasp the concept that, while OCD is part of her life, it doesn't have to define her. She started to realise that she could either continue to let OCD take away all her joy, or she could try to get on with life alongside it.

'She recently got her hair coloured for the first time, and she's started to put on some make-up for the first time. She didn't think she deserved to have any of that for a long time. Every parent says, "I just want my kids to be happy." And when they can't let themselves be happy, it's beyond distressing . . .' Rose trails off, momentarily drawn back into her parental nightmare.

'She's such a beautiful, empathetic person,' she continues, once she finds her way back to the present. 'She's always focused on other people. She thanks me for every single thing I ever do for her. But she can finally allow herself to be happy, which is a huge thing,' says Rose with a beaming smile.

Chapter 13

THE RIPPLE EFFECTS

Often when you have a mental illness, it's easy to think that your behaviour and your moods aren't affecting anyone around you. The alternative can be too much to bear: the idea that you're causing other people to suffer—when you think that it's only you targeted by the OCD—can be very hard to accept.

For this reason—and due to the fear of being labelled as weird or crazy—people with OCD will often try to hide their behaviours. They're prone to being perfectionists, so the idea of being thought of as 'less than' in any way can be terrifying.

While I didn't understand that I was experiencing OCD until I was well into adulthood, I knew instinctively to keep my obsessions and compulsions hidden from the wider world.

I was open with my parents, because I was suffering so much and needed their reassurance and support, but the thought of anyone else knowing what I was experiencing filled me with fear. And while my parents, particularly my mum, were subjected to my relentless, looping thoughts, I still tried to filter my level of day-to-day suffering so I didn't worry them too much. I wanted to be okay; my logic was that if I projected the image of being okay, perhaps this internal torture would recede at some point.

Once I was in my teens and OCD was overwhelming me, it became really tough for my parents because they didn't understand what was going on. I refused to see a therapist, so we were all stuck in this no-man's-land without any answers. They were unwittingly fuelling my OCD by accommodating my constant reassurance-seeking, and they couldn't understand why no amount of comfort or pacification would make a dent in my anxieties. I think this caused a feeling of helplessness; once I agreed to seek professional help, they were both enormously relieved.

HOW TO HELP A LOVED ONE WHO HASN'T YET SOUGHT HELP

If you have a loved one who is resisting treatment, please know that this is a normal and rational response to the threatening fears swirling in their head. However, the good news is that there's an increasing number of mental health professionals out there with experience in treating OCD. With the right amount of gentle encouragement and support, it's likely that your loved one will seek help when they're ready.

NORMALISE RECEIVING MENTAL HEALTH TREATMENT

In the last twenty years, a lot of work has been done to break down the stigmas associated with mental illness and seeking professional help. As a Millennial, I know more people who are regularly seeing a psychologist than people who aren't. The whole process has been demystified to a certain extent, which is a positive thing. However, there can still be a reluctance for some people. In this case, it can be helpful to talk to them about your own experience with a mental health professional (if you have it, and if it was positive), or the experiences of someone else you know, to make them feel less alone or ashamed.

In our household of three young kids, Hugh and I try to talk openly and honestly about our appointments with our 'Worry Doctors' (psychologists). We keep it age-appropriate and don't go into detail, but we're trying to normalise the process of seeking help to maintain good mental health, as we would to maintain good physical health. When my son asks me why I take a pill in the morning, I tell him it helps me to feel happier and less worried. Sometimes these things can feel hard to talk about, especially if you didn't grow up discussing these topics, but according to author and professor Brené Brown, secrecy, silence and judgement will only breed shame.[1]

FIND BOOKS/PODCASTS THAT WILL MAKE THEM FEEL LESS ALONE

Your loved one might not yet be diagnosed with OCD, but if you find any books, websites or podcasts that you think will resonate with their experience, gently encourage your loved one to seek them out in their own time. For more information, turn to the Resources section at the end of the book.

FIND A PROFESSIONAL WITH EXPERIENCE IN TREATING OCD

Once your loved one has agreed to see a mental health professional, make sure you find someone who has experience in treating OCD and using exposure and response prevention (ERP) therapy. Finding someone who is non-judgemental and knowledgeable about the ins and outs of OCD is important. Having a miserable first encounter can set the tone for someone who is already unsure about therapy, and it might put them off seeking help again.

TALK ABOUT ANONYMITY

It might be worth mentioning to someone who is resistant to therapy that any mental health professional is bound by ethical guidelines. Unless there's a significant risk of harm to their client or others, or they're subpoenaed to court, they must protect their client's privacy and keep all conversations confidential.

DISCUSS THE POSITIVES OF SEEKING HELP

It can be easy to focus on the negative feelings that can come up when considering therapy. It's good for people to know that seeking professional help can be life-changing. Talking to an expert can also be interesting, freeing and, yes, even fun (if you find the right person!). Personally, seeing a psychologist sometimes feels like I have access to a cheat sheet that others don't have. I have insights to questions that have always plagued me, and the ability to see myself in a fresh light. It's like a new dimension has opened up that I've never noticed before.

If they're worried about treatment feeling uncomfortable or unearthing negative feelings, gently remind them that the alternative also involves discomfort. As Thai Buddhist monk Ajahn Chah wrote, 'There is suffering you run away from, which follows you everywhere. And there is suffering you face directly, and in doing so become free.'[2] Psychologist Dr Jonathan Grayson encourages people to create a cost–benefit analysis if they're resisting treatment, because 'it reminds you that the alternative to recovery is also hell'.[3]

DON'T PUSH IT

You can't force anyone to seek help. Even if it's your child, there's sometimes only so much you can do to get a reluctant participant to sit in front of a therapist. It's hard because we *know* it would be beneficial for them, and we can't understand why they won't just take the leap. But that's the thing—it is a leap, and when you don't know if or how you're going to land, that can be really scary. Having empathy for their apprehension will help you, and them, to take things at their desired pace. If they're adamant that they don't want help, please don't give up on them. It doesn't mean they never will. Continue to gently encourage them, without any pressure. Your unwavering support is doing much more for them than you think.

THE FRUSTRATIONS OF LIVING WITH SOMEONE WHO HAS OCD

For many parents, siblings, friends and partners, living with someone who has OCD can be a constant struggle and a daily frustration. Obsessions and compulsions can occupy so much time and drain the energy of everyone in the house. Because people with OCD literally fear that something catastrophic is likely to happen if they don't perform certain rituals, they can be overcome with anger or distress if someone interferes with or tries to stop a compulsion.

If you don't have OCD, the obsessions and compulsions of your loved one will most likely seem odd at best, and downright insane at worst. You'll want to shake them out of it and tell them to stop worrying. *Just live your life, nothing bad will happen—and even if it does, your compulsions wouldn't change anything anyway! Just stop!*

One thing to remember is that the more you criticise someone with OCD, the stronger their anxiety is likely to become. No one *wants* to spend hours carrying out compulsions. It's important to see this behaviour as a symptom of an illness, not a personality trait. They despise OCD as much as you do, and they need your support to get the upper hand over it.

OCD is something I doggedly tried to conceal from friends and former partners. Despite my efforts, there would have been many instances when it was obvious that something was going on. Perhaps I seemed distracted, overly anxious or distant. I was always worried that if anyone managed to catch me mid-compulsion, then they would interrupt it or tell me to stop, and I wouldn't get the feeling of 'working something out' or a sense of completeness. So, if I was in a bad place with my OCD, I'd either avoid social situations or use a toilet cubicle or shower as a compulsion oasis.

OPENING UP

Once I met Hugh and it was clear to me that this was a serious relationship, I knew that I had to be open and honest with him. I'd matured a lot since my previous serious relationship, and while I wasn't formally diagnosed with OCD at that time, I did have an appreciation of what was going on in my head. Luckily, Hugh is not just understanding, but also proactively supportive as a partner. Having worked in the mental health industry for years and grown up with a sister with severe mental illness, he was empathetic and always jumped at the chance to learn more about OCD.

But it hasn't always been easy. Hugh is someone who always feels like it's his job to make people happier: to lift their mood

Signs of OCD

No matter how skilled someone is at concealing their OCD, there will always be signs to look out for:

- repetitive behaviours with chronic inflexibility
- prolonged periods of time spent alone (for example, in the bathroom or in their room)
- constant questioning and need for reassurance
- tasks taking longer than usual
- avoidance of places, situations, events or objects
- constant lateness and/or trouble leaving the house
- increased irritability, indecisiveness or anxiety.

and brighten their day. So, it's been difficult for him to not always be able to snap me out of my thoughts or lift me from the depressive daze that OCD tends to bestow upon me. For most of our relationship, I've been receiving professional help and taking medication, so things have been well managed, but it saddens me to think about the ways in which my mental illness has negatively affected him and caused him heartache.

One of the most helpful things we've done together is have a session with my clinical psychologist, Dr Andrea Wallace, so she could explain OCD to him and—more importantly—*my kind* of OCD. I'd always struggled to explain how my OCD played out, especially because a lot of the time I wasn't doing overt compulsions. But she was able to clarify it all for him in a detached, informative way that didn't carry the weight of emotion and frustration found in my explanations. This one session was transformative for our relationship, and I'd highly recommend doing something like this with a loved one if you get the chance.

Hugh and I have been living together for eight years, and in that time he's learned a lot. He knows far more than I do about living with someone who has OCD, so I asked him to offer his perspective and advice about how to support a loved one.

Hugh's insights

I was getting ready to head interstate for work for a couple of days. I had packed my bags and was saying my goodbyes to the kids, when I realised that I had no idea where Penny was. I was running late, so I recruited the kids to help me find her. After a brief and exciting (for the kids) search around the house, I was surprised to find her standing in our walk-in robe, in near darkness, staring at her phone, with a look of sheer panic on her face.

When I asked what was going on, she blurted out what I quickly realised was an obsessive and intrusive thought. I let out a sad and defeated sigh. She was in the grips of an obsessive loop. I had no idea where it had come from, nor did I have any idea how long she had been battling with it for. Suddenly, the thing that I couldn't possibly be late for took a back seat. *Okay, it's on, it's happening,* I thought to myself. I had gone over and over in my head what I was supposed to do when Penny was caught in an obsessive loop. But now, just like an actor on stage who had forgotten their lines, I had frozen right there in front of her. Finally, an important recollection came to me.

Whatever you do, do not reassure her. You know that's the last thing you're meant to do. No matter what she comes at you with, DO NOT REASSURE HER. Once again, Penny expressed her fear to me with a desperate look in her eye, like she was silently pleading for me to reassure her that she wasn't what her brain was telling her she was. So, what did I do? I reassured her that there was no way she was what her brain was telling her she was. 'You're not meant to reassure me,' she sobbed. *Oh my God, this is so bloody hard*, I thought desperately to myself. I'm not allowed to give her the one thing she so desperately wants right now.

In a panic, I attempted to give her a logical explanation for what she was obsessing over to fix the problem and make it go away. In doing so, I only made it worse. I can't properly recall what happened next, but I know the conversation ended with me holding her as she cried and cried in front of our then two-year-old daughter.

As I headed down the highway that night, I couldn't stop ruminating (ironically) on the fact that we had been together for over six years, and I still wasn't quite able to step up and help in her time of need.

I've shared this story because I'm about to give advice on how to be with someone who has OCD, and the last thing I want to do is appear like an expert who has all the answers. So, before I share the tips and strategies that have helped me, I just want to say this—it can be hard to live with someone who has OCD, and in trying to be there for Penny, I fail all the time. I know what to do in theory, but it can be very hard to put it into practice, under pressure, when the person you love most in the world is struggling, and they turn to you.

That said, I do have a few tips that I would love to pass on to others who are close to someone with OCD. They have proved to be very helpful for me and Penny.

Educate yourself

Read books, listen to podcasts and seek out everything you can on the topic. The more you learn about OCD, the less alone you'll feel. Loving someone with OCD can feel isolating, because try as they might, they just can't always be present with you. Realising that there are many other people out there struggling with OCD has helped me to think, *Well, I can't be the only person to have been through this lonely feeling.* I think it also means a lot to the person with OCD when they see you leaning into the condition and wanting to know more.

Hug it out

When they're really in a loop, and you can see that they're being tortured by their unrelenting thoughts, I always think they must be feeling a great deal of shame in that moment. In my experience, a physical embrace is the best way to communicate love, acceptance and support. It's important for them to know that, no matter how confronting their thoughts might feel, you aren't going anywhere.

Validate them

If they don't feel like being physically close to you, it's important to find a way to validate them. They need to feel loved in that moment. Don't try to fix the problem they're experiencing. It's futile. Instead, let them know that the way they're feeling makes sense. Saying things such as 'I totally understand why you feel that way' will help them to not feel silly or ashamed.

Don't give psychological advice

Having read all about OCD now, you'll be very tempted to give psychological advice. It comes from a very loving place, but it's not your role. Hopefully, they'll have a therapist for that. It also might come across as patronising.

Try not to take it personally

This is very much a case of do as I say, not as I do. I still find this one hard. If Penny is caught with a ruminating thought and just can't be present, it seems to me like I'm not worth her attention in that moment. When I manage to remind myself that it's got absolutely nothing to do with me and she can't help it, I cope a lot better.

Laugh out loud

When Penny laughs, two things happen. Firstly, her smile lights up the room, and secondly, she automatically becomes very present. When it's appropriate, if you can find a way to get your partner to laugh, you'll help them to escape their ruminating thoughts, even if only for a few moments, and it can be a much-needed respite for them. My only caveat to this is that you don't have to do it every single time you see them struggling. I have made this mistake all too often, and it's exhausting!

Privately celebrate the good days

You'll have days—maybe even weeks, months or years—when they've got a handle on their OCD. Make sure you really take that in and appreciate those moments. I don't often say to Penny, 'Gosh your OCD has been great of late', as I'm worried that her brain will see that as a challenge and start trying to sabotage the situation. I just make sure I really take in the good times and appreciate how lucky we are that things are going so well.

There is so much hope for people with OCD to get better with the right treatment and, crucially, the right support. I wouldn't be where I am today without the patience, love and understanding I've had from my family.

If you're supporting someone with OCD there will undoubtedly be good days and really bad days. Try not to get caught up in whether you are 'doing it right' or not. The most important thing is that you're there for them, even on their worst days. Especially on their worst days. When you have OCD you can often feel so alone and even abandoned by your own mind. For them to know that they will never be abandoned by those who they are closest to will bring them so much comfort, even if it's not obvious, or acknowledged. Please don't give up on them.

A FINAL WORD

I don't want the existence of this book to signify to anyone that I am 'fixed'. Writing a book while pregnant with my third child, and then during the postpartum period, unsurprisingly triggered stress and anxiety, which then caused my own OCD to flare up at times. Like most people who have a mental illness, I have good days and bad days. Sometimes I feel so far away from my OCD that I can almost make out the edges of it. I'm able to look at it with the same detachment as I would a passing cloud. But occasionally it will again descend on me, and suddenly I'm not looking at the cloud, I'm *in* the cloud, and I can't see anything clearly. It doesn't tend to last long but knowing that it can envelop me when I least expect it can be unnerving. I'm mentioning this because I want to normalise the inevitable ups and downs of living with OCD.

However, having been through the process of writing this book, my overwhelming feeling is one of hope. The cutting-edge research that is being done to understand more about why OCD occurs, and consequently how it can be treated, is cause for great optimism—for those already diagnosed as well as those who will be diagnosed in the future. Additionally, an increasing number of people are talking about, and advocating for, OCD in the public arena. This can only be a positive thing, and it will hopefully lead to less stigma and a more nuanced understanding of what it means to have OCD.

Whether you are someone who suffers from OCD, or you have a loved one who does, I hope this book has also given you some optimism.

OCD may have stolen your joy, but I guarantee you can get it back.

RESOURCES

HOTLINES AND CRISIS HELP

If a life is in danger, please call 000 immediately.

Beyond Blue: 1300 22 4636 or www.beyondblue.org.au
headspace: (03) 9027 0100 or https://headspace.org.au
Kids Helpline: 1800 55 1800 or https://kidshelpline.com.au
Lifeline: 13 11 14 or www.lifeline.org.au
Q Life (anonymous and free LGBTIQ+ peer support and
    referral): 1800 184 527 or https://qlife.org.au
Suicide Call Back Service: 1300 659 467 or
    www.suicidecallbackservice.org.au
13 YARN (Aboriginal and Torres Strait Islander crisis support
    line): 13 92 76 or www.13yarn.org.au

To find your local mental health crisis team, ring your closest major public hospital.

If you're not sure what to do, phone healthdirect on 1800 022 222.

For Child and Adolescent Mental Health Services (CAMHS), visit your state's health department website.

BOOKS

Fiction

John Green, *Turtles All the Way Down*, New York City, NY: Dutton Books, 2017

Memoir

David Adam, *The Man Who Couldn't Stop*, London: Pan Macmillan, 2014

Lily Bailey, *Because We Are Bad*, Kingston upon Thames: Canbury Press, 2016

Joanne Limburg, *The Woman Who Thought Too Much*, London: Atlantic Books, 2010

Shala Nicely, *Is Fred in the Refrigerator?*, Marietta, GA: Nicely Done, 2018

Various authors, *Try Not to Think of a Pink Elephant*, Fremantle, WA: Fremantle Press, 2022

General help

Jonathan S. Abramowitz, *Getting Over OCD* (2nd edn), New York City, NY: Guilford Press, 2018

Jonathan Grayson, *Freedom From Obsessive-Compulsive Disorder*, Los Angeles, CA: Penguin, 2003

Sally M. Winston and Martin N. Seif, *Overcoming Unwanted Intrusive Thoughts*, Oakland, CA: New Harbinger Publications, 2017

Self-compassion and mindfulness

Tara Brach, *Radical Acceptance*, New York City, NY: Random House, 2003

Joseph Goldstein, *Mindfulness*, Louisville, CO: Sounds True, 2013

Jon Hershfield & Tom Corboy, *The Mindfulness Workbook for OCD*, Oakland, CA: New Harbinger Publications, 2013

Jon Hershfield & Shala Nicely, *Everyday Mindfulness for OCD*, Oakland, CA: New Harbinger Publications, 2017

Jon Kabat-Zinn, *Wherever You Go, There You Are*, Westport, CT: Hyperion Press, 1994

David J. Keuler, *Healing from Obsessive-Compulsive Disorder*, Washington, DC: Guillon Press, 2019

Kristin Neff, *Self-Compassion*, New York City, NY: HarperCollins, 2011

Kimberley Quinlan, *The Self-Compassion Workbook for OCD*, Oakland, CA: New Harbinger Publications, 2021

Relationship OCD (ROCD)

Sheva Rajaee, *Relationship OCD*, Oakland, CA: New Harbinger Publications, 2022

Allison Raskin, *Overthinking About You*, New York City, NY: Workman Publishing Company, 2022

Acceptance and commitment therapy (ACT)

Russ Harris, *The Happiness Trap*, Boston, MA: Trumpeter, 2008

Families

Jonathan S. Abramowitz, *The Family Guide to Getting Over OCD*, New York City, NY: Guilford Press, 2021

Jo Derisley, Isobel Heyman, Sarah Robinson & Cynthia Turner, *Breaking Free From OCD*, London: Jessica Kingsley Publishers, 2008

Jon Hershfield, *When a Family Member has OCD*, Oakland, CA: New Harbinger Publications, 2015

Eli R. Lebowitz, *Breaking Free of Child Anxiety and OCD*, Oxford: Oxford University Press, 2020

John S. March, *Talking Back to OCD*, New York City, NY: Guilford Press, 2006

New parents

Karen Kleiman and Amy Wenzel, *Dropping the Baby and Other Scary Thoughts*, Abingdon: Routledge, 2020

Pamela S. Wiegartz & Kevin L. Gyoerkoe, *The Pregnancy & Postpartum Anxiety Workbook,* Oakland, CA: New Harbinger Publications, 2009

Kids and teenagers

Lily Bailey, *When I See Blue*, London: Hachette, 2022

Dawn Huebner, *What to Do When Your Brain Gets Stuck*, Washington, DC: American Psychological Association, 2007

Amita Jassi, *Can I Tell You About OCD?*, London: Jessica Kingsley Publishers, 2013

Kristina Sargent, *Mindful Games for Kids*, Oakland, CA:
    Callisto Media, 2020
Joe Wells, *Touch and Go Joe*, London: Jessica Kingsley
    Publishers, 2006
Chris Wever, *The Secret Problem*, Concord West, NSW:
    Shrink-Rap Press, 1996

WEBSITES

International OCD Foundation (IOCDF): https://iocdf.org
Made of Millions: www.madeofmillions.com
NOCD: www.treatmyocd.com
OCD BOUNCE: https://ocd.org.au
OCD Center of Los Angeles (OCDLA): https://ocdla.com
ROCD.net: https://rocd.net
So OCD: https://soocd.com.au

ONLINE SUPPORT AND INFORMATION
FOR PERINATAL OCD

Centre of Perinatal Excellence (COPE): www.cope.org.au
Maternal OCD: https://maternalocd.org
Mums Matter Psychology: www.mumsmatterpsychology.com
Perinatal Anxiety & Depression Australia (PANDA):
    1300 726 306 (Monday to Saturday) or
    https://panda.org.au
Postpartum Support International: www.postpartum.net
The Parent-Infant Research Institute (PIRI): www.piri.org.au

PODCASTS

All The Hard Things
AT Parenting Survival Podcast
Breaking the Rules: A Clinician's Guide to Treating OCD
The OCD Chronicles
The OCD Stories
Your Anxiety Toolkit

WEBINARS

AT Parenting Survival (free webinars): www.anxioustoddlers.
    com/webinars
Melbourne Wellbeing Group ('Treating OCD: Breaking the
    Cycle at Home' by Dr Celin Gelgec and Dr Victoria Miller):
    www.melbournewellbeinggroup.com.au/webinars-and-books
UCLA Center for Child Anxiety Resilience Education and
    Support (CARES) ('Childhood OCD'): https://carescenter.
    ucla.edu/childhood-ocd-webinar

INPATIENT OPTIONS

The Melbourne Clinic: (03) 9429 4688 or
    https://themelbourneclinic.com.au/services/
    inpatient-programs/obsessive-compulsive-disorder-program

GROUP THERAPY AND SUPPORT GROUPS

Anxiety Recovery Centre Victoria (ARCVic) OCD support
    group: www.arcvic.org.au/our-services/zoom-support-groups

Melbourne Wellbeing Group: www.melbournewellbeinggroup.
  com.au/group-therapy
OCD Online Group Program: www.melbpsych.com.au/
  ocd-online-group-therapy-melbourne-australia
OCD STOP Program (Swinburne University): www.
  mentalhealthonline.org.au/pages/about-the-ocd-stop-program
WayAhead OCD online support group: https://
  understandinganxiety.wayahead.org.au

ONLINE OCD PROGRAMS

Adults

CBT School: www.cbtschool.com
MindSpot: www.mindspot.org.au/course/ocd
This Way Up: https://thiswayup.org.au/programs/ocd-program

Kids and teens

OCD? Not Me!: www.ocdnotme.com.au

APPS

Exposure—Face Your Fears
GGOC: OCD Relief
NOCD: OCD Therapy and Tools

TV SHOWS AND MOVIES

You Can't Ask That: OCD (ABC iView)
Pure (Stan)
UNSTUCK: An OCD Kids Movie: www.ocdkidsmovie.com

YOUTUBE CHANNELS

Dr Russ Harris—Acceptance Commitment Therapy:
  www.youtube.com/channel/UC-sMFszAaa7C9poytIAmBvA
Natasha Daniels (OCD therapist):
  www.youtube.com/@Natashadanielsocdtherapist

NOTES

PREFACE

1 J. Grayson, *Freedom from Obsessive-Compulsive Disorder*, Los Angeles, CA: Penguin, 2003, p. xiii.

2 D.D.J. Cooper, I.E. Perkes, J. Lam-Po-Tang, et al., 'Finding help for OCD in Australia: Development and evaluation of a clinician directory', *Australian Psychologist*, 2023.

3 S. Ziegler, K. Bednasch, S. Baldofski & C. Rummel-Kluge, 'Long durations from symptom onset to diagnosis and from diagnosis to treatment in obsessive-compulsive disorder: A retrospective self-report study', *PLoS ONE*, 2021, vol. 16, no. 12.

CHAPTER 1: THE ONSET

1 American Psychiatric Association, *Diagnostic and Statistical Manual of Mental Disorders*, Fifth Edition Text Revision (DSM-5-TR), p. 10.

2 American Psychiatric Association, DSM-5-TR, p. 11.

3 American Psychiatric Association, DSM-5-TR, p. 11.

4 American Psychiatric Association, DSM-5-TR, p. 12.

5 American Psychiatric Association, DSM-5-TR, p. 12.

6 E. Toro-Martínez, 'Trastorno obsesivo compulsivo y trastornos relacionados: Un nuevo capítulo en el DSM-5' [DSM-5: OCD and related disorders], Vertex, 2014, vol. 25, no. 113, pp. 63–7.

7 American Psychiatric Association, DSM-5-TR, p. 6.

8 PsychDB, 'Obsessive-Compulsive Personality Disorder (OCPD)', 2023, <www.psychdb.com/personality/obsessive>, accessed 28 April 2023.

9 B. Van Noppen, 'Obsessive Compulsive Personality Disorder (OCPD)', International OCD Foundation (IOCDF), 2010, <https://iocdf.org/wp-content/uploads/2014/10/OCPD-Fact-Sheet.pdf>, accessed 28 April 2023; OCD UK, 'Obsessive Compulsive Personality Disorder (OCPD)', 2023, <www.ocduk.org/related-disorders/obsessive-compulsive-personality-disorder/>, accessed 28 April 2023; PsychDB, 'Obsessive-Compulsive Personality Disorder (OCPD)'.

10 Van Noppen, 'Obsessive Compulsive Personality Disorder (OCPD)'.

11 Van Noppen, 'Obsessive Compulsive Personality Disorder (OCPD)'.

12 Grayson, *Freedom from Obsessive-Compulsive Disorder*, pp. 8, 9.

13 Grayson, *Freedom from Obsessive-Compulsive Disorder*, p. 11.

14 D.L. Pauls, 'The genetics of obsessive-compulsive disorder: A review', *Dialogues in Clinical Neuroscience*, 2010, vol. 12, no. 2, pp. 149–63.

15 C. Jones, 'Queensland researchers at QIMR Berghofer find likely cause of obsessive-compulsive disorder', *ABC*, 18 April 2023, <www.abc.net.au/news/2023-04-18/ocd-research-queensland-qimr-berghofer/102231932>, accessed 24 April 2023.

16 Grayson, *Freedom from Obsessive-Compulsive Disorder*, p. 17.

17 Grayson, *Freedom from Obsessive-Compulsive Disorder*, p. 20.

18 D.J. Keuler, 'A Big Bang theory of OCD: Why the first few moments make all the difference in the world', International OCD Foundation, 2020, <https://iocdf.org/expert-opinions/a-big-bang-theory-of-ocd-why-the-first-few-moments-make-all-the-difference-in-the-world/>, accessed 1 May 2023.

19 Keuler, 'A Big Bang theory of OCD'.

20 D. Adam, *The Man Who Couldn't Stop*, London: Pan Macmillan, 2014, pp. 16, 57–60.

21 Keuler, 'A Big Bang theory of OCD'.

CHAPTER 2: THE PEAK

1 Adam, *The Man Who Couldn't Stop*, p. 20.

2 M. Ingle, 'Obsessive Compulsive Disorder', *You Can't Ask That*, ABC TV, 2021.

3 Ingle, 'Obsessive Compulsive Disorder'.

CHAPTER 3: THE FIRST TRY

1 Mojo Crowe, <www.youtube.com/watch?v=nr9YTsLw-Goo&t=280s>, accessed 24 April 2023.
2 K. Quinlan, *The Self-Compassion Workbook for OCD*, Oakland CA: New Harbinger Publications, 2021, p. 29.
3 D.J. Keuler, *Healing from Obsessive-Compulsive Disorder*, Washington, DC: Guillon Press, 2019, p. 114.
4 Keuler, *Freedom from Obsessive-Compulsive Disorder*, p. 44.
5 Grayson, *Freedom from Obsessive-Compulsive Disorder*, p. 35.
6 Quinlan, *The Self-Compassion Workbook for OCD*, p. 39.

CHAPTER 4: THE INTERLUDE

1 S. Bareilles, *We Can Do Hard Things*, podcast, October 2022.
2 IOCDF, 'Medications for OCD', 2023, <https://iocdf.org/about-ocd/ocd-treatment/meds/>, accessed 24 April 2023.
3 IOCDF, 'Medications for OCD'.
4 Australian Government Department of Health and Aged Care, 'Citalopram and heart problems: Changes to recommend doses', 2011, <www.tga.gov.au/news/safety-alerts/citalopram-and-heart-problems-changes-recommended-doses>, accessed 24 April 2023.

CHAPTER 5: THE SILENCE

1 Vipassana meditation, 'About the technique', 2023, <www.dhamma.org.au/meditation.htm>, accessed 24 April 2023.

2 J. Hershfield & S. Nicely, *Everyday Mindfulness for OCD*, Oakland, CA: New Harbinger Publications, 2017, p. 14.
3 Hershfield & Nicely, *Everyday Mindfulness for OCD*, p. 13.
4 Hershfield & Nicely, *Everyday Mindfulness for OCD*.
5 Hershfield & Nicely, *Everyday Mindfulness for OCD*, p. 31.

CHAPTER 6: UPS AND DOWNS

1 E. Sharma & S.B. Math, 'Course and outcome of obsessive-compulsive disorder', *Indian Journal of Psychiatry*, 2019, vol. 1, supplement 1, pp. S43–S50.
2 H. Naftalovich, G.E. Anholt, R. Keren, et al., 'Waxing and waning: The roles of chronotype and time of day in predicting symptom fluctuations in obsessive-compulsive disorder using a daily-monitoring design', *Journal of Psychiatric Research*, 2021, vol. 143, pp. 91–7.
3 S.A. Green & B.M. Graham, 'Symptom fluctuation over the menstrual cycle in anxiety disorders, PTSD, and OCD: A systematic review', *Archives of Women's Mental Health*, 2022, vol. 25, pp. 71–85.
4 OCD Center of Los Angeles, 'OCD vs. GAD and How to Tell the Difference', 10 July 2019, <https://ocdla.com/ocd-vs-gad-7071>, accessed 2 May 2023.
5 Beyond Blue, 'Anxiety', 2023, <www.beyondblue.org.au/the-facts/anxiety>, accessed 2 May 2023.
6 C.R. Reynolds & R.W. Kamphaus, *Generalized Anxiety Disorder*, 2013, <http://images.pearsonclinical.com/images/assets/basc-3/basc3resources/DSM5_DiagnosticCriteria_GeneralizedAnxietyDisorder.pdf>, accessed 26 April 2023.

7 OCD Center of Los Angeles, 'OCD vs. GAD and How to Tell the Difference'.

8 J. Abramowitz, 'OCD and Depression', IOCDF, 2010, <https://iocdf.org/expert-opinions/ocd-and-depression/>, accessed 2 May 2023.

9 Abramowitz, 'OCD and Depression'.

10 Hershfield & Nicely, *Everyday Mindfulness for OCD*.

11 B. Smale, 'Obsessive Compulsive Disorder', *You Can't Ask That*, ABC TV, 2021.

12 L. Fernández de la Cruz, M. Rydell, B. Runeson, et al., 'Suicide in obsessive-compulsive disorder: A population-based study of 36 788 Swedish patients', *Molecular Psychiatry*, 2017, vol. 22, pp. 1626–32.

CHAPTER 7: THE CIRCUIT BREAKER

1 Royal College of Psychiatrists, 'Perinatal OCD', 2021, <www.rcpsych.ac.uk/mental-health/problems-disorders/perinatal-ocd>, accessed 26 April 2023.

2 N. Hudepohl & M. Howard, 'Perinatal OCD: What research says about diagnosis and treatment', undated, <https://iocdf.org/expert-opinions/perinatal-ocd-what-research-says-about-diagnosis-and-treatment>, accessed 26 April 2023.

3 N. Fairbrother, F. Collardeau, A.Y.K. Albert, et al., 'High prevalence and incidence of obsessive-compulsive disorder among women across pregnancy and the postpartum', *Journal of Clinical Psychiatry*, 2021, vol. 82, no. 2, 20m13398.

4 J.E. Brumbaugh, C.T. Ball, J.E. Crook, et al., 'Poor neonatal adaptation after antidepressant exposure during the third trimester in a geographically defined cohort', *Mayo Clinic*

Proceedings: Innovations, Quality & Outcomes, 2023, vol. 7, no. 2, pp. 127–39.

CHAPTER 8: THE TREATMENT

1 A. Funder, *All That I Am*, Sydney: Penguin Random House, 2012, p. 295.
2 IOCDF, 'Exposure and Response Prevention (ERP)', 2023, <https://iocdf.org/about-ocd/ocd-treatment/erp/>, accessed 2 May 2023.
3 IOCDF, 'Exposure and Response Prevention (ERP)'.
4 L.M. Koran, G.L. Hanna, E. Hollander, et al., 'Practice guideline for the treatment of patients with obsessive-compulsive disorder', *Psychiatry Online*, 2007, <https://psychiatryonline.org/pb/assets/raw/sitewide/practice_guidelines/guidelines/ocd-1410197738287.pdf>, accessed 2 May 2023.
5 J.S. Abramowitz, 'The psychological treatment of obsessive-compulsive disorder', *The Canadian Journal of Psychiatry*, 2006, vol. 51, no. 7, pp. 407–16.
6 Grayson, *Freedom from Obsessive-Compulsive Disorder*, p. xv.
7 P.L. Fisher & A. Wells, 'How effective are cognitive and behavioral treatments for obsessive-compulsive disorder? A clinical significance analysis', *Behavior Research and Therapy*, 2005, vol. 43, no. 12, pp. 1543–58; Koran, et al., 'Practice guideline for the treatment of patients with obsessive-compulsive disorder', p. 12.
8 Grayson, *Freedom from Obsessive-Compulsive Disorder*, p. 42.

CHAPTER 9: ROCD AND ME

1   S. Rajaee, *Relationship OCD*, Oakland, CA: New Harbinger Publications, 2022, p. 8.

CHAPTER 10: THE REVELATION AND THE RELAPSE

1   S. Pappas, 'Group therapy is as effective as individual therapy, and more efficient. Here's how to do it successfully', *Monitor on Psychology*, American Psychological Association, 2023, vol. 54, no. 2, <www.apa.org/monitor/2023/03/continuing-education-group-therapy>, accessed 2 May 2023.
2   C. Maye, K. Wojcik, A. Candelari, et al., 'Obsessive compulsive disorder during the COVID-19 pandemic: A brief review of course, psychological assessment and treatment considerations', *Journal of Obsessive-Compulsive and Related Disorders*, 2022, vol. 33.
3   Hershfield & Nicely, *Everyday Mindfulness for OCD*, pp. 155–65.

CHAPTER 11: THE FUNNY SIDE

1   Hershfield & Nicely, *Everyday Mindfulness for OCD*, pp. 113–14 (emphasis in original).

CHAPTER 12: KIDS AND OCD

1   J.S. March, *Talking Back to OCD*, New York City, NY: Guildford Press, 2006, p. 75.
2   Pediatric OCD Treatment Study (POTS) Team, 'Cognitive-behavior therapy, sertraline, and their combination for

children and adolescents with obsessive-compulsive disorder:
The Pediatric OCD Treatment Study (POTS) randomized
controlled trial', *JAMA*, 2004, vol. 292, no. 16,
pp. 1969–76.

3 March, *Talking Back to OCD*, p. 73.

4 March, *Talking Back to OCD*, p. 76.

5 March, *Talking Back to OCD*, p. 74.

6 IOCDF, 'Medication for Pediatric OCD', undated,
<https://kids.iocdf.org/what-is-ocd-kids/how-is-ocdtreated/
medication-for-pediatric-ocd>, accessed 1 May 2023; March,
Talking Back to OCD, p. 73.

7 March, *Talking Back to OCD*, p. 74.

CHAPTER 13: THE RIPPLE EFFECTS

1 B. Brown, *Listening to Shame*, March 2012. Available at:
<www.ted.com/talks/brene_brown_listening_to_shame/c>,
accessed 1 June 2023.

2 Ajahn Chah, cited in Keuler, *Healing from Obsessive-Compulsive Disorder*, p. 53.

3 Grayson, *Freedom from Obsessive-Compulsive Disorder*,
p. 115.

ACKNOWLEDGEMENTS

I want to express my heartfelt gratitude to all the wonderful people who trusted me to tell a part of their story in this book. It's a brave thing to allow someone to capture vulnerable moments of your life in print for the benefit of others. I couldn't include all the stories I wanted to, but I appreciate all who offered to help and shared parts of their life with me. You are courageous and inspiring, and I learned so much from each one of you.

This book would not have been written without the encouragement and support of my publisher, Tessa Feggans. You are wonderful at your job and I will always owe you a debt of thanks for giving me this opportunity. You took a gamble on an emotionally fragile pregnant woman who had never written a book, and I am very grateful to you. Also, a big thankyou to Angela and the rest of the team at Allen & Unwin.

An enormous thankyou to my beautiful husband, Hugh. You have put up with a lot, and yet you are the most eternally loving and encouraging partner—a one-man cheer squad. Thank you for always delighting in the happiness and success of everyone around you. I love you very much and couldn't have completed this book without you.

To my mum, Anne, and dad, Rob, thank you for being a gentle safety net throughout my life. You are the ones who taught me how to love and be loved. Both of you always made me feel safe in the world, no matter how scary things felt in my mind. I thank my lucky stars that I have you as parents—you inspire me to be the best parent I can to my kids.

To my wonderful brother, Nick. Ever since I was a little girl, when you tried to convince your teacher to let me join your class, you have been a safe haven for me. Having you around to offer advice throughout this process has been a great help and comfort. Thank you for letting me include parts of your story in this book. You are the best brother and the most present, loving uncle.

To Liz, Richard, Josh, Soph and Georgia, I love and admire you all greatly. I've been incredibly lucky to inherit another beautiful family through Hugh. Thank you for going to such lengths to help us with the ongoing juggle of work and kids. You always do it so lovingly and we just couldn't survive without you.

Trying to write a book while pregnant with my third child would have been impossible without a village of people surrounding me. Annie, we would be lost without you, and I can't believe we've been lucky enough to find someone as wonderful as you to help to keep our kids fed, loved and dancing when Hugh and I aren't around. To the Naroon crew, thank you for your constant friendship and support (and Clint, a big thankyou for your legal expertise).

A huge thankyou to all the wise experts I interviewed to gain a better understanding of OCD. Your knowledge and passion have given me hope and optimism for the future.

To Andrea, I can't properly articulate how much you have changed my life for the better. I hope that one day you will write a book so that all your wisdom is captured in print. Thank you for using your intellect, passion, and empathy to help me, and countless others.

To the beautiful members of my OCD group, who I have laughed, cried and cringed with (while performing ERP therapy), you have all become close friends and confidants. I'm grateful to know you all.

Finally, to my kids, Benji, Elsie and Patrick, thank you for reminding me why I need to put in the work to get better. Being a good parent is always my top priority, and being present for the joys and challenges of parenthood is a gift I will never underestimate. I love you all so very much.

Penny is a writer, OCD advocate, mum of three tiny people and social work student. She has a background in media and communications and has previously worked as a communications specialist in the mental health, non-profit and health communications sectors. Penny has a Masters of Global Media Communications and co-created the website soocd.com.au to help others to navigate the world of OCD.

She lives in Melbourne with her kids, husband and a disastrously naughty black Labrador.